This book should be returned to any branch of the
Lancashire County Library on or before the date shown

Lancashire County Library
Bowran Street
Preston PR1 2UX

Lancashire
County Council

www.lancashire.gov.uk/libraries

COUNTRYSIDE BOOKS
NEWBURY BERKSHIRE

First published 2003
© Nick Burton 2003

COUNTRYSIDE BOOKS
3 Catherine Road
Newbury, Berkshire

09135527

To view our complete range of books,
please visit us at
www.countrysidebooks.co.uk

ISBN 1 85306 726 1

To My Dad

Designed by Graham Whiteman
Maps and photographs by the author

Typeset by Techniset Typesetters, Newton-le-Willows
Produced through MRM Associates Ltd., Reading
Printed by Woolnough Bookbinding Ltd., Irthlingborough

Contents

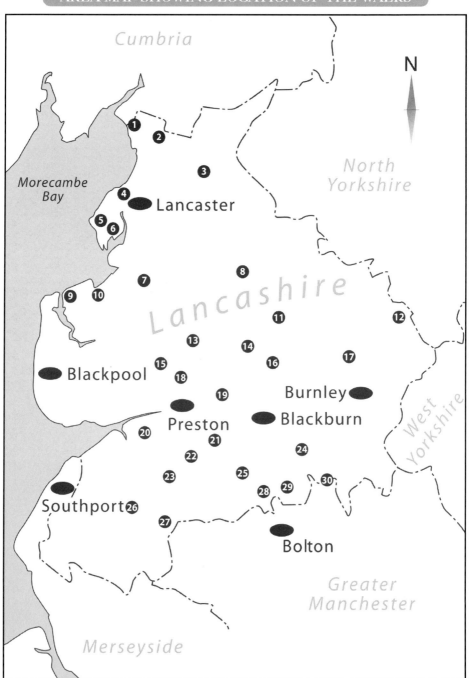

PUBLISHER'S NOTE

We hope that you obtain considerable enjoyment from this book; great care has been taken in its preparation. Although at the time of publication all routes followed public rights of way or permitted paths, diversion orders can be made and permissions withdrawn.

We cannot, of course, be held responsible for such diversion orders and any inaccuracies in the text which result from these or any other changes to the routes nor any damage which might result from walkers trespassing on private property. We are anxious though that all details covering the walks are kept up to date and would therefore welcome information from readers which would be relevant to future editions.

The simple sketch maps that accompany the walks in this book are based on notes made by the author whilst checking out the routes on the ground. They are designed to show you how to reach the start, to point out the main features of the overall circuit and they contain a progression of numbers that relate to the paragraphs of the text.

However, for the benefit of a proper map, we do recommend that you purchase the relevant Ordnance Survey sheet covering your walk. The Ordnance Survey maps are widely available, especially through booksellers and local newsagents.

Lancashire is undeniably a county of contrasts: from the wooded limestone fringes of the Lake District to the edge of the Manchester conurbation; from breezy promenades and salty estuaries to boggy Pennine moors and crags. The short walks in this collection cover the whole variety of landscapes to be found in this Red Rose region. There are strolls over the high fells of Bowland, the mudflats of Morecambe Bay, the lush pastures and hedgerows of the Ribble Valley, and wild Pendle. The Pennine crags and the flat plain of rural West Lancashire are also featured.

The villages of Lancashire are as diverse as its landscapes. There are the pre-Domesday linear street villages like Waddington, Grindleton and Pendleton and the holiday hotspots of Silverdale, Hest Bank and Knott End. The walks also visit the medieval market centres of Chipping and Goosnargh; Belmont and Kelbrook that were once thriving weaving and textile villages; and the commuter country of old Croston and 'new' Forton. Added to all these is Roman Ribchester, with its tales of famous kings like Henry VI and James I.

There is little doubt that the best way to explore Lancashire's fine villages is on foot. Only by walking their ancient tracks and admiring their historic buildings can you sense their true character. Similarly, their pubs can offer the visitor a slice of true village life. In this collection of strolls we visit roadside inns, old coaching houses, simple farmhouses converted into pubs and hostelries that have for centuries been the focus of village society. Pub names themselves can be revealing. It is not surprising that we encounter the Dolphin Inn by the coast, the Shoulder of Mutton in sheep farming country and two Buck Inns on the edge of Bowland Forest.

This collection of strolls is a good introduction to walking in the county and all the walks should be well within the capabilities of the novice walker who has a reasonable level of fitness. I hope you gain as much enjoyment from these walks as I have had in devising them. Where possible, within each chapter, I have given alternative suggestions for car parking rather than pub car parks so that these can be left free for other patrons. However, if you do intend to leave your car in the pub car park whilst you walk, it is only courteous to speak with the landlord before you set off.

So, happy strolling!

Nick Burton

Silverdale
The Royal

MAP: OUTDOOR LEISURE 7 THE ENGLISH LAKES (SE) (GR 458749)

WALK 1

DISTANCE: 4$\frac{1}{2}$ MILES

DIRECTIONS TO START: LEAVE THE A6 AT CARNFORTH AND FOLLOW THE SIGNED MINOR ROADS VIA WARTON WHICH LEAD INTO THE VILLAGE. **PARKING:** START THE WALK AT THE SHORE ROAD CAR PARK WHICH IS JUST DOWNHILL FROM THE VILLAGE MAIN STREET. THERE IS A SIGN FOR THE SILVERDALE HOTEL AT THE TOP OF THE SHORE ROAD AND THE ROAD ENDS AT THE CAR PARK.

Silverdale is a mix of holiday flats, caravan parks and residential homes set against an enchanting backdrop of limestone woodlands, coastal cliffs and salt marshes. Within only a few square miles, the area offers a variety of excellent walking and the views across Morecambe Bay to the Lake District have made it fashionable with holidaymakers since Victorian days.

The walk begins along the shore and heads for the Cove. It then passes Arnside Tower, a 15th century pele tower built as a defence against invading Scots and follows a variety of woodland tracks through Eaves Wood before crossing fields back to the village.

The Royal

The Royal or Royal Hotel – as it offers accommodation – is both a lively village local and holidaymakers' pub. Situated in the heart of the village it dates from the mid-19th century, a time when the newly-opened railway from Hest Bank to Grange began to bring tourists to this little visited limestone coast. The area quickly caught on as a holiday centre and retirement retreat for Lancashire and Yorkshire folk and, not surprisingly, Victorian mansions were built along the wooded hills. Old prints and memorabilia now adorn the cosy Royal which has an open plan lounge bar, separate restaurant and beer garden. In addition to the regular menu there are daily blackboard specials and traditional regional dishes. Food is served all day Sundays and lunchtimes and evenings on every other day. There is also traditional John Smith's Bitter. Telephone: 01524 701266.

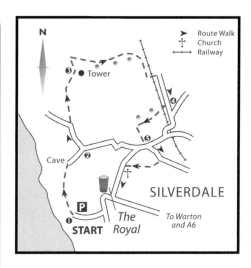

The Walk

① From the car park walk along the shore path passing below the row of cottages to your right. There is a view across the bay to the town of Grange-over-Sands. The path soon leads to a small rocky cove and a cave in the cliffs indicated by a large circular hole. Leave the shore here by following the track to the right of the cave which leads to a wooden field gate leading onto a lane. The lane leads up to a junction with another road.

② Turn left and follow this road, signposted for Arnside. After about 250 yards the road starts to bend left by a footpath sign. Join this path to Silverdale Road and Far Arnside on the right and go straight ahead through the caravan park. Keep going in the same direction and another sign for Arnside Tower is passed. The path leads down the caravan driveway (Elm Grove) passing a children's play area on your right. When the road starts to bear right towards more caravans, leave it and go straight ahead under telegraph lines to join a grassy tree-lined track. This leads directly to Arnside Tower.

③ Go through the gate to the Tower then follow the track downhill towards the farmhouse. Do not go through the gate to the farm but turn sharp right along the path signed for Middlebarrow. This leads to a gate (the higher of two gates) at the entrance to a wood. Go through this and a track through the dense wood is now followed for about $\frac{1}{2}$ mile, leading to a railway crossing. Stop, look and listen before crossing as this is the line between Silverdale and Arnside. Continue straight

The coastal path to Silverdale Cove

ahead down the lane and follow it as it turns right past cottages until it reaches a set of white gates on the right indicating another railway crossing. A path is signed here for Waterslack and Eaves Wood.

④ Cross the railway again and follow the track around to the left until it reaches the garden centre car park and entrance sign. At this point turn right by a gate and go through the gap in the wall to enter Eaves Wood. Bear left and when the path forks by a wall gap, take the right fork uphill. Keep going straight ahead along a track following the woodland edge. After passing a second yellow waymarker post take the left fork and when the path shortly forks again, take the left fork, dropping downhill from the main track to reach a wall corner. An enclosed path now leads to the road.

⑤ Cross the road and directly opposite go up Bottoms Lane. When the road bends left follow the footpath on the right, signed for St John's church. Go straight ahead from here along the wall side, passing through two more white gates to reach a path junction by cottages. Turn right here and the track leads to the main village street. Turn left to reach the pub and shops and when the road turns sharp left, turn right to follow the shore road downhill back to the shore car park.

PLACES OF INTEREST NEARBY

Follow the brown tourist road signs for just a short distance from Silverdale to arrive at the RSPB's **Leighton Moss Nature Reserve** (telephone: 01524 701601). This extensive reedbed reserve offers a chance to see wildlife including bitterns, marsh harriers and otters and also has a popular visitor centre.

Yealand Conyers
The New Inn

MAP: OUTDOOR LEISURE 7 THE ENGLISH LAKES (SE) (GR 504748)

WALK 2

DISTANCE: 2 MILES

DIRECTIONS TO START: YEALAND CONYERS IS 2 MILES NORTH OF JUNCTION 35 OF THE M6 AT CARNFORTH. IT IS SIGNED WESTWARDS OFF THE A6 AND IS SITUATED ALONG THE MINOR ROAD LINKING WARTON WITH ARNSIDE. **PARKING:** APART FROM THE PUB REAR CAR PARK (CUSTOMERS), THERE IS VERY LIMITED PARKING IN THE VILLAGE.

Hidden along the hedge-lined back roads from the busy A6, it is not surprising that the 'Yealands' villages of Redmayne and Conyers were a focus for secret Quaker meetings in the 17th century. The movement's leader, George Fox, preached here in 1652 and the Friends' Meeting House and Quaker school remain a part of the village's heritage today. But the settlement itself is much older and the ancient township of the 'jalant' – the Anglo-Saxon name for 'high ground' – was recorded in the Domesday Book. Adam Conyers was the lord of the manor and, around the village, remnants of the medieval field system remain.

The walk climbs along the wooded slopes of Cringlebarrow Wood from where there are extensive views north to the Lake District. The route returns to the New Inn on a section of the medieval field path which links the villages of Conyers and Redmayne.

The New Inn

In fact, the inn is not so 'new'. It was new in the 17th century when it was built to replace the village's original hostelry which was destroyed by the Roundheads during the English Civil War. Shame on those Puritans! Thankfully, the replacement inn is a hidden gem. The ivy-clad exterior almost makes it go unnoticed to drivers passing through the village. But this is deceiving, for inside you will discover a popular country pub with oak beams and welcoming log fires in winter. Home-made fresh local food is available both as bar snacks and as part of the à la carte menu offered in the restaurant. Families are welcome and tasty food is served every day from 12 noon until 9.30 pm. Beer connoisseurs should note, this is a Hartleys of Ulverston pub with the traditional 'beers from the wood' including the strong Hartleys XB Bitter. You will also find Robinsons seasonal bitters and Hatters Mild – rare in these parts. And, of interest to ghost hunters, the inn is reputedly haunted. But then, no self-respecting old oak-beamed country inn is really complete without a resident spook! Telephone: 01524 732938.

The Walk

① Outside the New Inn walk uphill along the main village street for a short distance until Dykes Lane is passed on the left. At this point, climb steps to join the footpath on the right hand side of the road. Walk diagonally left uphill through the parkland with good views looking north. Go through the gate at the top of the hill.

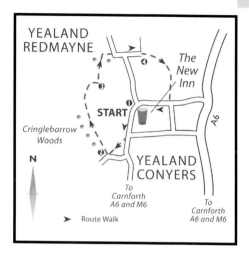

② Turn right after the gate and follow the footpath signs heading directly to a gate leading into the wood above the lower track. This leads to another gate and a path signed for Yealand Redmayne. Follow this path all the way to the opposite side of the field where you will find a gate, squeeze stile and footpath signpost. Cross the stile and continue straight ahead here alongside the wall until another gate is reached. Enter the field and bear right around the wall corner to go through another gate in a wall.

③ Enter woodland again and follow the main path which bears left and passes through the wood to reach a wall stile at the edge of a field. Cross this and

PLACES OF INTEREST NEARBY

The impressive Georgian country house of **Leighton Hall** (telephone: 01524 734474) is just ½ mile away from the village. There are antiques and fine art collections to be found inside the house and numerous events held out on the lawns throughout the year including regular bird of prey flight displays.

Yealand's medieval field system

drop downhill with a view of Yealand Conyers to your right. At the road turn right and continue straight ahead down Well Lane when the road turns sharp right. On a clear day, the Yorkshire peak of Ingleborough can be seen directly ahead.

④ At the end of the lane go straight ahead at the gate to a private access, then immediately right over a stile in the fence. The path crosses two fields and then follows a hedged track When the lane is reached turn right, then left along the village main street to reach the pub.

Wray
The George & Dragon

DIRECTIONS TO START: WRAY IS 8 MILES NORTH-EAST OF LANCASTER, ON THE B6480. FROM LANCASTER, FOLLOW THE A683 FROM JUNCTION 34 OF THE M6 AND TURN ONTO THE B ROAD AFTER PASSING THROUGH CLAUGHTON. **PARKING:** LIMITED PARKING ON THE MAIN VILLAGE STREET WHICH RUNS OFF THE B ROAD PAST THE GEORGE AND DRAGON TO A BRIDGE OVER THE ROEBURN. THERE IS MORE ROOM TO PARK AT THE UPPER END OF THE VILLAGE STREET CLOSE TO THE BRIDGE.

Wray nestles sleepily above the confluence of the Rivers Roeburn and Hindburn in a patchwork of woodland and fields backed by the high fells of Bowland and the Yorkshire Dales. A close inspection of the village reveals picturesque 17th and 18th century stone cottages, historic buildings like the Quaker Meeting House and Captain Pooley's School and a bridge over the tranquil river. In short, Wray is an undiscovered gem that does not reveal its charm very easily to the passing motorist. Its narrow alleys, cobbles and field paths are ideal territory for the walker.

This walk encircles the village along a variety of field paths, tracks and lanes. It starts by the bridge over the River Roeburn, passes its meeting point with the River Hindburn then follows a back lane before climbing south of the village to give panoramic views to the Yorkshire Dales and the Pennines and across the Lune Valley to the Lake District.

The George and Dragon

Hard to believe that the village of Wray once had seven inns! But in centuries past it was a bustling community that thrived on sheep farming and traditional rural industries like weaving, basket making and oak crafts. When the wind whistled off the wild fells and down through the woods of Roeburndale, you could bet there was always a welcoming light and fire at the George and Dragon. There still is today and the inn remains a hearty haven for a 'modern' mix of travellers and locals. There is something quintessentially English about pubs with the traditional name 'George and Dragon'. Overlooking the cobbles of the village main street, Wray's historic inn has the warm ambience and old-fashioned feel you would expect to find in a typical Lunesdale country hostelry. An extensive full menu and bar snacks are on offer (no meals on winter Mondays) together with Boddingtons Bitter and the traditional cask ales of the local Lancaster brewery, Mitchell's. There is a pleasant beer garden, and overnight accommodation is also available. Telephone: 015242 21403.

The Walk

① Start from the George and Dragon and walk up the village street past the church and post office. The road bends left and comes to a bridge over the River Roeburn. Do not cross it but turn left along the signed public footpath leading along the river bank. The path skirts woodland, passes through a gate and stile and follows the edge of a large field alongside the river, eventually reaching a wide road verge by a bridge.

② Cross the road directly here to join an access track that leads to a signed bridleway along a high-hedged lane. This bridleway (Back Lane) is followed between fields for the next $3/4$ mile before it reaches the road again. Continue straight ahead to your right along the road for a short distance until a crossroads is reached. Turn left at the crossroads along the lane signed for Roeburndale West.

PLACES OF INTEREST NEARBY

A few miles north up the Lune Valley, via the A683, head for Arkholme village and follow the signs by the Bay Horse Inn for Docker. Here can be found **Docker Park Farm** (telephone: 01524 221331) which offers a working farm experience with lots for kids to get involved in. Feed the lambs, collect the eggs, enjoy a tractor ride and visit the owl sanctuary and visitor centre. The centre is closed to the public in winter.

The peak of Ingleborough above Wray village

③ The lane leads uphill and is followed for the next ¹/₂ mile until a footpath signpost and stile are reached on the left hand side. Join this path and follow the field edge along the fence side, crossing the stile at the opposite side of the field to follow the edge of another field. The path leads alongside woodland and gives fine views eastwards to the Three Peaks of the Yorkshire Dales. Pass through field gates to rejoin a lane above the village.

④ Follow the lane downhill past the school and it reaches the main village street by the post office. Turn left for the George and Dragon.

Hest Bank
The Hest Bank

MAP: EXPLORER 296 LANCASTER, MORECAMBE & FLEETWOOD (GR 468667)

WALK 4

DISTANCE: 4½ MILES

DIRECTIONS TO START: THE VILLAGE IS SITUATED ALONG THE A5105 COASTAL ROAD BETWEEN MORECAMBE AND CARNFORTH. **PARKING:** START THE WALK FROM THE SEAFRONT CAR PARK WHICH IS OPPOSITE STATION ROAD AND ACCESSED ACROSS THE RAILWAY LEVEL CROSSING BY THE SHORE CAFÉ.

Hest Bank appears a genteel dormitory village but its history is caught up in the folklore and legends of Morecambe Bay. It was from the coastal bank here that horse and carriages set off on the perilous crossing to Furness and there are centuries of tales of lives lost upon the treacherous quicksand. The Lancaster Canal of the 1790s and the 1846 railway cut across the edge of the salt marshes but it was only in the 20th century that modern Hest Bank developed as a 'ribbon' of affluent residential development between the A6 and the coast road.

This attractive low-lying walk follows easy gradients and combines the coastal path with the canal towpath. It heads north to Bolton-le-Sands with panoramic views north across the bay, then returns to Hest Bank via the Lancaster Canal.

The Hest Bank

Though the leisure craft moored along the adjacent Lancaster Canal have brought a new breed of customer to the Hest Bank, this popular hostelry had a former existence as a coaching inn dating from the 16th century. It was from here that carriages set off across the sands to Furness and the inn always provided a guiding light to the travellers crossing Morecambe Bay. The multi-roomed, stone-built inn now attracts coach parties of day trippers flocking to the coast together with the canal trade – the 1980s' addition of a conservatory to the original stone building is testament to its appeal. The beer garden lawn runs down to the canal moorings and is packed with visitors in summer. Good food is served from 12 noon until 9 pm every day and there is a varied list of daily specials and a children's menu. The Hest Bank is also renowned for its selection of chargrilled prime British steaks. Horse riders and walkers are all welcome. Hand-pumped Boddingtons Bitter, Tetley's Mild, Robinsons Best and Timothy Taylor Landlord are all available. Telephone: 01524 824339.

The Walk

① From the end of the car park continue north along a shoreline track until another car parking area is reached by a farm. Continue straight ahead alongside the stone wall to reach a stile in a wall by a Lancashire Coastal Way signpost. Cross the wall, climbing uphill to panoramic views, then drop down to cross a stile and enter a small caravan park. Bear left around the caravans and cross over another stile in a narrow gap between a wall and Red Bank Farm. Go straight ahead along the coast path until a road is reached by cottages.

② Pass the cottages and keep to the road as it turns sharp right uphill and crosses the railway. The road winds past residential avenues before reaching the A6. Cross the road with care and go up the lane directly opposite which soon reaches the Lancaster Canal. Turn right, go down the steps and join the canal towpath here, turning right along it.

③ Follow the towpath for the next $1\frac{1}{4}$ miles alongside pretty gardens until bridge number 118 is reached. At this point you can leave the canal and turn left over the bridge to reach the Hest Bank inn. But then rejoin the towpath and continue straight ahead past the canal moorings. After passing under canal bridge number 117 turn right along a track, climbing wooden steps to a black metal kissing gate. Go straight ahead

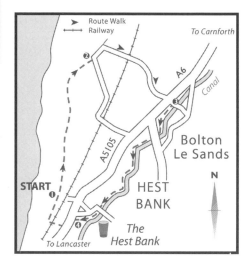

Warton Crag overlooking Morecambe Bay

between gardens, cross a residential avenue and continue straight ahead along a narrow path which drops to the coast road.

④ Turn left along the road for a short distance, cross over by a pillar box and bus stop and follow the steps which lead to a bridge over the railway. Cross the railway and the path emerges on the shore. Turn right here and follow the coastal path

PLACES OF INTEREST NEARBY

Just north along the A6 is the market town of **Carnforth** which is well known for its secondhand book shop and the train station which was the setting for the famous movie romance *Brief Encounter*.

between the salt marsh and the railway embankment back to the shore car park.

Heysham
The Royal Hotel

MAP: EXPLORER 296 LANCASTER, MORECAMBE & FLEETWOOD (GR 412615)	**WALK 5**	**DISTANCE:** 1¼ MILES

DIRECTIONS TO START: FOLLOW THE SIGNS OFF THE A589 COASTAL ROAD FOR HEYSHAM VILLAGE. **PARKING:** USE THE PAY AND DISPLAY CAR PARK BY THE BUS TURNING AREA ADJACENT TO THE SHOPS ON THE MAIN VILLAGE STREET.

Hidden behind Heysham's busy port and nuclear power station is a surprisingly historic and attractive village of pretty whitewashed cottages and rocky shores. The craggy promontory of Heysham Head is now owned by the National Trust and it was here that St Patrick landed, according to legend, after being shipwrecked on his crossing from Ireland. The ruined chapel with its stone graves open to the elements dates from the 6th century and Viking invaders also landed here a few centuries later. The chapel and crags are a solitary and spiritual place in an area predominantly given over to good old-fashioned holiday-making.

This short walk is a mini-discovery of historic Heysham. It follows a roadside path before joining the track which leads to the coastal cliffs of Heysham Head and St Patrick's Chapel and returns to walk up the village main street to pass the pub.

The Royal Hotel

This whitewashed Mitchell's hostelry dominates the sea-end of the main village street and attracts day trippers strolling down to the open cliffs of Heysham Head. The beer garden and the street-front tables are a magnet for holidaymakers in the sunshine, but with beer festivals and local events the long-established hotel remains popular all year round. There is cask Mitchell's Bitter from the local Lancaster brewery and good home-cooked fare with a varied menu. Families are welcome and the hotel is open all day for food. Telephone: 01524 859298.

PLACES OF INTEREST NEARBY

Morecambe is Heysham's brash and breezy big brother and offers traditional resort entertainments like amusement arcades and seafront shops together with stunning views across Morecambe Bay. Why not have your photo taken with Eric Morecambe on the prom as a statue of the town's most celebrated son is now a very popular attraction (Morecambe tourist information centre, telephone: 01524 582808).

The Walk

① From the car park turn left and pick up a tarmac path which runs parallel to the road. This heads uphill away from the village and passes a cul-de-sac, Kintyre Way. Soon after this, cross the road via

The 6th century chapel of St Patrick

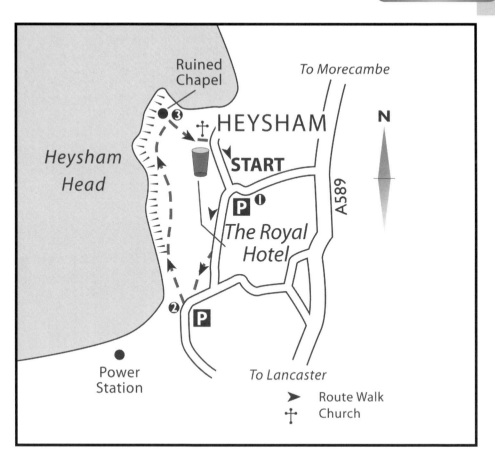

Route Walk
✝ Church

steps and join the footpath signed for Smithy Lane which runs across two grass fields and through a wall gap, heading for the car park by the power station.

② Opposite the car park, turn sharp right to follow the adjacent signed footpath along the shore. Either follow the shore edge of the field or the shore itself to reach a wooden kissing gate in a wall. If you have walked along the shore, climb the steps which lead back to the field edge. You have now entered the National Trust property of Heysham Head. A good

track here leads through another wall gap to the grassy promontory which offers fine views north across Morecambe Bay. All tracks lead to the ancient chapel remains. Don't miss the stone slab graves looking out to sea.

③ From the chapel follow the cobbled lane down past St Peter's church and bear right along the village street leading to the Royal Hotel. Continue straight ahead from here past the shops to return to the car park.

Overton
The Ship Hotel

MAP: EXPLORER 296 LANCASTER, MORECAMBE & FLEETWOOD (GR 437580)

WALK 6

DISTANCE: 2 MILES

DIRECTIONS TO START: FROM THE A683 BETWEEN LANCASTER AND HEYSHAM, FOLLOW THE SIGNS FOR THE VILLAGE WHICH LEAD DOWN A MINOR ROAD TO THE VILLAGE CROSSROADS. **PARKING:** ROADSIDE PARKING IN THE VILLAGE.

The splendid isolation of Overton, perched above the mudflats of the Lune Estuary, has helped preserve its old-fashioned character. The river and the sea were for centuries the only real link between Overton and the outside world as the village boats sailed over to Glasson and Lancaster. Coastal tides once lapped against the whitewashed fishermen's houses of the village until land was reclaimed in the 18th century. The partly Saxon and Norman church overlooking the

shore at Overton had a light and a bell to guide shipping at night. The bell also came in useful to warn of Scottish marauders!

This walk combines the village's quiet hedged back lanes and the pebbly shoreline of the estuary to provide a short expedition of amazing variety. It encircles the shore then climbs to Hall Greave – a perfectly shaped hill, little in size but big on views – offering an unparalleled panorama from the Pennines to the Lake District.

The Ship Hotel

This sturdy seafaring hostelry looms large on the village high street and has no doubt been a welcome sight for generations of Lunesdale fishermen returning from the sea with their full nets of salmon. The Victorian hotel still has an original mosaic tiled floor and tile-topped tables. It also has old-fashioned bird egg collections and stuffed birds to remind you that you are in prime sea bird-watching country. The traditional Thwaites house offers quality home-cooked fare for seafarers, bird-watchers, ramblers, holidaymakers, children and passing Vikings. Food is served all week at lunchtimes and in the evenings and there is a beer garden, also pool and darts. Telephone: 01524 858231.

PLACES OF INTEREST NEARBY

Having viewed historic **Lancaster** from a distance, it is also worth visiting close at hand. Just 5 miles east of Overton, the old county capital has many visitor attractions. Tour the Norman Lancaster Castle, the 17th century Judge's Lodgings and the skyline folly of the Ashton Memorial for starters (Lancaster tourist information centre, telephone: 01524 32878).

crossing a cattle grid to follow a farm track. When the track soon bends around to the right, continue straight ahead to go through a kissing gate which leads to the shore. Follow this to the right and cross a stile in front of the cottage. There are fine views across the estuary to Lancaster, Bowland and Glasson Dock from here. Follow the path below the cottage wall, just keeping to the shoreline as it skirts around the promontory to a gate.

The Walk

① Starting from the Ship Hotel walk downhill along the main village street to a crossroads. Turn right here along Chapel Lane (signed for the church) and the road swings left past a shop. Keep on this lane for about ¼ mile until it swings sharp left to Church Grove. Go straight ahead at this point along the route (Bazil Lane) signed for Sunderland Point Road.

② Follow the track between hedges and continue straight ahead,

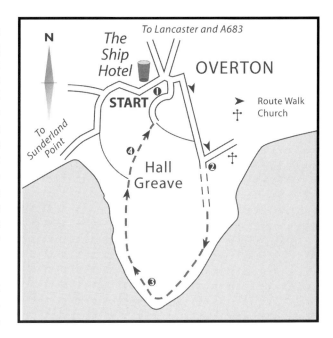

Across the Lune Estuary towards Glasson

③ Go through the gate and simply continue along the shoreline, heading for a white-painted ladder stile in the distance straight ahead. Leave the shore at the ladder stile and cross it to climb uphill through fields. Cross more ladder stiles to reach the white trig point at the top of the low hill. The views from here are breathtaking, particularly north to the Three Peaks of Yorkshire and the Lake District fells.

④ Continue in the same direction from the summit along the path to the ladder stile, signed 'Back Street 150 yards'. Cross the stile and follow a hedged path which leads to another path junction. Turn left here and follow the track slightly downhill between a wall and houses. Keep to this track which crosses a residential avenue and eventually reaches Chapel Lane alongside the shop. Turn left and left again to rejoin the main village street.

Forton
The New Holly

MAP: OUTDOOR LEISURE 41 FOREST OF BOWLAND OR EXPLORER 296 LANCASTER, MORECAMBE AND FLEETWOOD (GR 490513)

WALK 7

DISTANCE: 3¼ MILES

DIRECTIONS TO START: THE VILLAGE IS LOCATED JUST OFF THE A6 BETWEEN GARSTANG AND LANCASTER. HEADING NORTH, TURN FIRST LEFT OFF THE A6 AFTER PASSING THE NEW HOLLY INN. IT IS ALSO JUST A FEW MILES SOUTH OF THE M6, JUNCTION 33. **PARKING:** TURNING OFF THE A6, ALMOST IMMEDIATELY THERE IS A PUBLIC CAR PARK NEXT TO THE VILLAGE RECREATION GROUND.

Forton has a confusing split personality. It dates back to Domesday but also gives its name to an M6 service station. To the east of the A6 it has old-fashioned cottages; to the west of the A6 it has modern suburban housing and playing fields. It has an inn called the 'New Holly' but where is the 'Old Holly'? Forton's dichotomy is largely a result of the route of the north-south A6 which has created two almost separate communities, one either side of the busy road. Old Forton lies to the east of it along Hollins Lane

whereas a modern residential extension to the village has developed to the west of the A6 and doubled the size of the local population.

This circuit unites the two sides of the village and comprises a gentle stroll across fields, lanes and along the winding towpath of the Lancaster Canal. The New Holly inn on the A6 is reached roughly halfway along the walk. The route then passes through the old village and returns to the car park of the 'new' village along paths through pastures.

The New Holly

Meet me in the Holly! That would have been a confusing thing to say in the past since Forton had four inns which were, namely: the Old Holly, Middle Holly, New Holly and … the Holly! Had they all still existed today taxi drivers would have a nightmare! Judging by its name, the one surviving inn was not the first of the 'Holly's. But it has taken on the role of its predecessors as a staging post for modern-day travellers on the north-south A6 road. Children are welcome and the hostelry now provides traditional home-cooked food every day from 12 noon until 8 pm. There are also cask Thwaites ales. Telephone: 01524 793500.

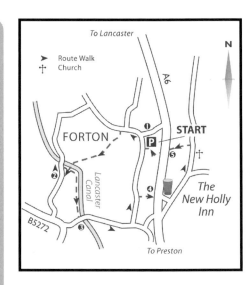

The Walk

① From the car park entrance turn left and walk along the street through the village past the war memorial and school. Shortly a footpath is reached on the left hand side, signed for the Lancaster Canal. Go through the gates here past a pond and turn right to follow the field edge to a footbridge. Bear diagonally left here to cross another stile in the opposite field corner. From here bear slightly right across a large field with the Lancaster Canal directly ahead. Go through the gate and follow the track which crosses a bridge over the canal, then continue along the track, bearing right to join a lane.

② Turn right along the lane and this leads back to the canal at another bridge. Drop down to the towpath here and turn right, crossing under the road bridge and continuing along the towpath for about $^1/_2$ mile. Leave the canal by steps at the next road bridge, number 75 – Ratcliffe Bridge.

③ Turn left and cross the road bridge and follow the lane for about $^1/_4$ mile until it reaches a junction with another lane on the left. Turn left up Winder Lane and just before a farm is reached look out for signed footpaths in the hedges on either side of the lane. Take the footpath on the right hand side which crosses stiles and two fields and emerges on the A6 in the car park of the New Holly inn.

④ Cross over the A6 with great care. To continue the walk go down the track to the right hand side of the pub, then turn left on the adjoining lane which is now followed for about $^1/_2$ mile. After passing the post office and church turn left up the access to the Duchy of Lancaster Estate alongside a white cottage. Continue straight ahead through the gates and follow the field edge back to the A6.

The Lancaster Canal

⑤ Take great care re-crossing the A6 and directly opposite continue along a shady, conifer-lined path to a stile. Bear right to another stile then left along the edge of the playing field to the lane. Turn right along the lane, then right again to return to the car park.

PLACES OF INTEREST NEARBY

Just 4 miles south along the A6 is the historic market town of **Garstang** offering opportunities for shopping, drinking and eating. There is an over-abundance of hostelries here, a relic of its former importance as a meeting place for farmers from the Lancashire moors and plain. The busy market day is Thursday (Garstang tourist information centre, telephone: 01995 602125).

Newton
The Parkers Arms

MAP: OUTDOOR LEISURE 41 FOREST OF BOWLAND (GR 697504)

WALK 8

DISTANCE: 2 MILES

DIRECTIONS TO START: NEWTON VILLAGE IS 6 MILES NORTH OF CLITHEROE VIA THE B6478. **PARKING:** LIMITED ROADSIDE PARKING IN THE VILLAGE. THE PARKERS ARMS HAS A CAR PARK FOR PATRONS.

A marvellously preserved stone village of 17th and 18th century houses, Newton is situated in that part of the Hodder Valley that was administratively within the West Riding of Yorkshire prior to 1974. Newton predates the Domesday Book and also lies slap bang in the middle of the medieval unit of territory known as the Forest of Bowland. The 'forest' had its own laws and a court at neighbouring Slaidburn whilst one of Bowland's most important families are the Parkers who still reside at nearby Browsholme Hall and gave their name to Newton's inn. In the 17th century, the Quaker movement was alive and flourishing in Newton and its legacy survives in the village's Friends' Meeting House and the Old School.

This walk heads south from the village across the River Hodder and follows old field paths and lanes before returning to the river downhill across pastures. It is a walk through lush pastoral country but there are views to the nearby higher hills of Bowland.

The Parkers Arms

The brightly coloured flower displays outside this listed 18th century country inn are a welcoming sight to visitors on entering the village of Newton from the south. Add this to the lawn beer garden which looks down to the nearby bridge over the River Hodder and the unexpected rare breeds animal corner and it is not surprising that the Parkers Arms draws in visitors like a magnet. The inn is firmly rooted in the rural life of Bowland and the family coat of arms in question is depicted on the sign adorning the front of the building with its distinctive arch windows and doors. The Parker family shield includes the symbols of the stag and the two bowmen which hark back to the old days of the hunting forest. Inside this Whitbread inn you can relax by the open fire in winter, and throughout the year enjoy a large selection of home-cooked local food – at lunchtimes and in the evenings from Monday to Friday and from 12 noon until 9 pm at weekends. The pets corner alongside the pub should keep the whole family entertained.

Telephone: 01200 446236.

Looking towards the hills of Bowland

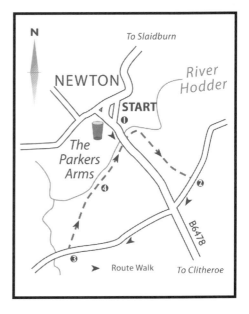

The Walk

① From the centre of the village walk downhill past the Parkers Arms and cross the road bridge over the River Hodder. Immediately on the left hand side go over the step stile by the gate and walk through the field, heading straight for the river. Bear right and cross a stile to follow a field edge heading slightly uphill. Go through gates to reach a lane.

Newton Bridge

② Turn right on the lane and walk to its junction with another road. Turn left then immediately right to go down the lane, signposted for Cow Ark. This lane is now followed downhill for about $^1/_2$ a mile until a disused farm building by a large conifer tree is reached at the bottom of the hill.

③ Just before the access gate to the building, look out for a stile and footpath signpost in the hedge on the right hand side of the road. Go over the stile and bear right uphill across the middle of the field to reach a stile and gate at the opposite field boundary. Go through this and bear slightly left downhill to another gate and stile. Continue in the same direction

PLACES OF INTEREST NEARBY

A few miles north-east of Newton is the ideal picnic area. **Stocks Reservoir** is reached off the B6478 beyond Slaidburn village and offers informal recreational opportunities including nature trails and cycle routes around the reservoir and Gisburn Forest.

downhill to join the river bank.

④ Cross further stiles straight ahead, one of which leads through a gap in a stone wall and leads to the riverside. With the river to your left, walk back to the road bridge. Turn left at the road to retrace your steps to the village.

Knott End-on-Sea
The Bourne Arms

(**MAP:** EXPLORER 296 LANCASTER, MORECAMBE & FLEETWOOD (GR 348485))

WALK 9

(**DISTANCE:** 2 MILES)

DIRECTIONS TO START: THE VILLAGE IS SITUATED AT THE END OF THE B5270 AND IS 2 MILES WEST OF THE A588 RUNNING BETWEEN HAMBLETON AND COCKERHAM. **PARKING:** FREE PARKING ALONG THE PROMENADE BETWEEN THE BOURNE ARMS AND THE VILLAGE CENTRE. ALTERNATIVELY, THERE IS A LARGE CAR PARK BEHIND THE COASTGUARD STATION FURTHER ALONG THE ROAD FROM THE BOURNE ARMS.

Knott End is a curious residential outpost perched on the coastal edge of vast acres of reclaimed rural mossland. It is cut off from the rest of Lancashire's holiday coast and the industry of Fleetwood by the silty estuary of the meandering River Wyre. There is a little ferry linking Fleetwood to Knott End which brings in the summer visitors but pleasures at Knott End are conducted at a sedate quiet place. Its main attractions are its village charm and the extensive views looking north from the long breezy promenade.

This short walk hardly leaves the confines of the village but still manages to capture the essence of Knott End. From the sea promenade it follows a suburban avenue to the rural mosses, then a green lane past Hackensall Hall to the cliff top golf course overlooking the estuary.

The Bourne Arms

This distinctive black and white building commands a prominent position along the promenade, close to the coastguard station and the ferry crossing to Fleetwood. Long before the coastguard came to town the Bourne Arms Hotel was a significant landmark for incoming trawlermen heading back to the calmer waters of the Wyre Estuary. Built as a hotel in 1846, the pub takes its name from the Bourne family who built it and resided at Hackensall Hall. It now attracts holidaymakers and day trippers in great numbers and provides friendly service and good home cooking. Meals are served at lunchtimes and in the evenings from Monday to Saturday and from 12 noon until 9 pm on Sundays. Beers available include Boddingtons Bitter, Flowers Bitter and Timothy Taylor Landlord Bitter. Telephone: 01253 810256.

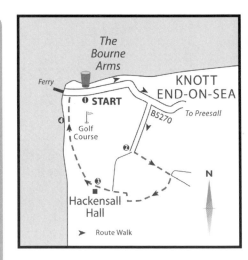

around the back of houses and becomes a woodland path. Go straight ahead through the woodland until a crossroads of tracks is reached between fields. Turn sharp right here and follow the wide, hedged track which swings right and heads back towards woodland. A signpost is reached indicating 'Knott End $^3/_4$ mile'. Ignore the track bearing right but go straight ahead to reach Hackensall Hall on your left.

The Walk

① From the Bourne Arms walk back towards the centre of the village along the seafront promenade. When the road bends around to the right, leave the seafront and follow the road past the shops in the centre of the village. Follow the main road through the village to the left then cross over and turn right down Hackensall Drive. Follow this residential road for about $^1/_4$ mile until it becomes a dead end.

② Turn sharp left along the signed public footpath by the end houses. This leads

PLACES OF INTEREST NEARBY

The port of **Fleetwood** is a stone's throw away from Knott End across the River Wyre. The little ferry service takes you there quickly and also provides a pleasant boat trip. If the ferry is not available, Fleetwood can be approached in a longer way via the road crossing of the Wyre at Shard Bridge. Visitors now flock to Fleetwood for the Freeport Village shopping experience (telephone: 01253 877377). Fleetwood also offers traditional seafront amusements, a famous market, leisure centre, floral gardens and trams which lead down the coast to Blackpool (Fleetwood tourist information centre, telephone: 01253 773953).

The Wyre Estuary

③ Keep the Hall and its outbuildings on your left and walk around the side of it before turning right at a waymarker post indicating the 'Wyre Way'. Follow the hedge side and then bear diagonally left across the golf course as indicated by the signpost. Head directly for the garage on the opposite side of the fairway. Turn right at the garage and follow the track at the edge of the course until a cottage is reached on the left.

④ Turn left immediately after passing the cottage and then right to follow the sea wall overlooking the estuary and looking across to Fleetwood. Pass the coastguard station and the ferry point and follow the road back to the Bourne Arms and promenade.

Pilling
The Golden Ball

MAP: EXPLORER 296 LANCASTER, MORECAMBE & FLEETWOOD (GR 404484)

WALK 10

DISTANCE: $2\frac{1}{2}$ MILES

DIRECTIONS TO START: TAKE THE A588 BETWEEN HAMBLETON AND COCKERHAM. ROUGHLY HALFWAY BETWEEN THESE TWO VILLAGES, FOLLOW SIGNS ON THE NORTH SIDE OF THE ROAD FOR PILLING. THE MAIN ROAD INTO THE VILLAGE LEADS TO THE POTTERY ON THE LEFT. **PARKING:** OPPOSITE THE POTTERY IS A FREE VILLAGE CAR PARK BY PUBLIC TOILETS AND A PLAYGROUND.

Proud Pilling provides a welcome burst of floral colour for much of the year amidst the flat grey landscape of the Fylde mosses. The low-lying flood bank overlooking Pilling Marsh may not be the most dramatic stretch of the Lancashire coast but the views north to Morecambe Bay certainly make it worth the excursion. The reclaimed marshes – which have literally shifted Pilling inland – are now a haven for wading birds. The village itself is a typical Fylde settlement, dominated by intensive agriculture which provided produce that was once moved by a local train line (now disused) between Garstang and Knott End.

This walk leads along the main village street and follows a quiet lane at the edge of the reclaimed marsh. It then joins the flood bank, taking in the extensive coastal views looking north before returning inland.

The Golden Ball

The sprawling red-brick Golden Ball was built in 1904 and maintains the traditional features of the Edwardian hotel it started life as: high ceilings, a long bar and large public and lounge rooms. In its dominant position on a village junction sandwiched between the moss and the marsh, it is a popular busy local but offers a friendly welcome to the many visitors who descend here in search of quality food like the traditional ample Sunday roasts. There is a beer garden, a children's play area and even a bowling green to keep all members of the family entertained. Bar meals are served at lunchtimes and in the evenings for most of the week and all day on Saturday and Sunday (note that the pub is closed Monday to Wednesday afternoons). Thwaites cask mild is included in a large selection of beers and spirits. Telephone: 01253 790212.

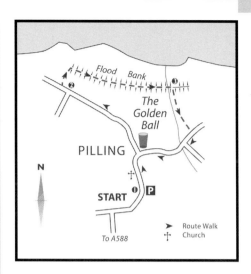

The Walk

① From the car park turn right along the main village street and follow the pavement to the junction overlooked by the Golden Ball. Turn left here along Fluke Hall Lane which passes the village school. This lane is now followed for nearly ³/₄ mile and leads out onto the marsh. Shortly after passing the adjoining

A blooming village sculpture

The old mill in Pilling is now a private residence

Wheel Lane on your left, look out for a gate and signpost on your right.

② Turn right off the road here along the concessionary footpath following a track which soon crosses a drain and leads onto the flood bank. Turn right along the raised bank and head eastwards with Pilling Marsh down to your left. Walk as far as the crossing point over a wide drain.

③ Turn right off the flood bank after crossing the drain and drop down to a track which heads back inland with Pilling church almost directly ahead. The track runs below the raised drain bank and leads to a road. Turn right along the road and cross the bridge over the drain. The road swings right then leads back to the Golden Ball. Retrace your steps to the car park from here.

PLACES OF INTEREST NEARBY

Glasson is north from Pilling along the coastal road and is a historic port with a colourful marina in the basin of the Lancaster Canal. There is an assortment of pubs and cafés here and a disused railway has been transformed into a recreational footpath which leads to a coastal picnic site at Conder Green.

Grindleton
The Buck Inn

MAP: OUTDOOR LEISURE 41 FOREST OF BOWLAND (GR 759455)

WALK 11

DISTANCE: 2 MILES

DIRECTIONS TO START: LEAVE THE A59 CLITHEROE BYPASS AT CHATBURN AND GRINDLETON VILLAGE IS A MILE NORTH OF CHATBURN VILLAGE. **PARKING:** THERE IS AMPLE ROADSIDE PARKING CLOSE TO THE PUB IN THE CENTRE OF GRINDLETON.

Like many of the other settlements that nestle in the lower folds of the Bowland Fells and brooding Pendle Hill, Grindleton is a picture perfect linear village. Its long main street links the higher ground at the 'Top of Town' to the crossing point over the River Ribble and the legacy of industrial mills can still be found along Grindleton Brook which feeds into Lancashire's chief river. Grindleton takes great pride in its long history and a trail leads around the lanes of the village, passing along the way the 1862 Methodist Free church and handloom weavers' cottages.

The village heritage is explored in this stroll which crosses Grindleton Brook and follows an old green lane between farmhouses. There are fine views over towards Pendle for most of the way before the route heads back to the pub.

The Buck Inn

Ramblers are so welcome at the friendly Buck Inn that they have even been given their own room! Colourful hanging baskets of flowers adorn the outside of the 17th century roadside inn for most of the year and it has won awards for not just its cuisine but also its fine appearance. Part of the Pubmaster chain, the Buck Inn is a traditional rustic hostelry with cosy rooms, wintertime log fires, wooden beams and a toby jug collection. There is a large selection of bar meals offering country fare or you can dine à la carte in the restaurant. Specialities include fresh fish and traditional roast dinners and beers on offer include John Smith's Smooth and Tetley Bitter. There is also a separate family dining area. Food is available at lunchtimes and in the evenings every day of the week. Telephone: 01200 441248.

PLACES OF INTEREST NEARBY

The remains of **Sawley Abbey** on the banks of the River Ribble are a place for quiet contemplation. The 12th century Cistercian abbey was founded by the white monks from Fountains Abbey in Yorkshire and the site is now managed by English Heritage. The abbey is situated on the south banks of the Ribble in Sawley village which is only a mile north-east of Grindleton.

② Cross the stile and turn right. This old green lane is now followed for about $1/2$ mile and winds its way gradually uphill to farmhouses. The view soon opens up looking south to the distinctive whaleback of wild Pendle Hill. Continue past the farmhouses until the lane forks into two.

③ Bear right along the tarmac lane here and it winds downhill to the brook before climbing again to the top end of Grindleton village. Turn right to follow

The Walk

① Start from the road junction between the Buck Inn and the Duke of York pub that literally face each other. Walk past the Duke of York but instead of following the road downhill almost immediately take the signed footpath on the right hand side of the road. This begins as a lane past cottages and drops downhill to a gate by an old mill on the brook. Go through the gate and climb the hill before turning sharp left to reach a stile in the fence. This leads to a stone stile and gate.

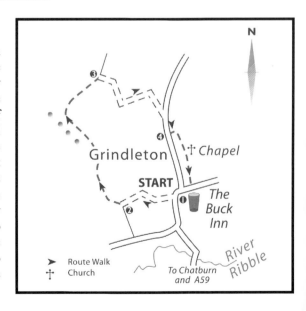

Looking south to Pendle Hill

the village high street. After about 250 yards, when the road starts to drop downhill, look out for a signed public footpath on the left hand side by a house with a large gable end.

④ Leave the road here and the path runs up a drive and swings right between stone walls. This path runs parallel to the main village street and drops down to the old Methodist church. Continue straight ahead along the stony track from here and at the road junction turn right to reach the pubs. An information board at the corner of the junction outlines the village history.

Kelbrook
The Craven Heifer

MAP: OUTDOOR LEISURE 21 SOUTH PENNINES (GR 903447)

WALK 12

DISTANCE: 3 MILES

DIRECTIONS TO START: THE VILLAGE IS SITUATED ON THE A56 HALFWAY BETWEEN COLNE AND EARBY. AT THE CRAVEN HEIFER, TURN RIGHT OFF THE A56 INTO A MINOR LANE LEADING TO THE CHURCH AND THE VILLAGE. THE WALK STARTS AT THE BECK BY THE CHURCH. **PARKING:** THERE IS AMPLE PARKING ON THE ROADSIDE ALONG THE MAIN VILLAGE STREET AT THE BACK OF THE A56.

Hiding in the shadow of the busy A56, Kelbrook is a little known village and so comes as a pleasant surprise. Turn off the main road to discover an old stone bridge over Harden Beck and St Mary's parish church which has a clock face on all four sides of its steeple. 'Chelbroc' is recorded in the Domesday survey but much of its growth came with the 18th and 19th century occupations of weaving and quarrying, in addition to traditional pastoral farming.

The walk follows the Pendle Way out of the village and heads eastward onto the Pennine moors along the valley of Harden Beck. Farm tracks and boggy paths across rough pasture take you on a mini-circuit around the valley, returning along a quiet moorland road offering views across to Pendle Hill and the Yorkshire Dales.

The Craven Heifer

The inn sign and name remind us we are on the edge of the Yorkshire Dales as the 'Craven Heifer' is a common pub name across this part of the Pennines. The 'heifer' in question was the legendary one ton calf born at nearby Gargrave in the Craven district in 1807! This Craven Heifer is proud of its local heritage, and old prints and memorabilia adorn the walls of the many rooms of the sprawling, friendly pub. The selection of drinks and meals is just as extensive as the pub and the former roadside farmhouse is a popular port of call for both travellers and locals. Food is available at lunchtimes and in the evenings every day of the week. Telephone: 01282 843431.

direction, crossing another ladder stile, and walk in the direction of the nearest farmhouse on the hillside ahead. This leads to a gate.

② At this point do not continue along the field edge but go straight ahead across the field until a stile in the next wall boundary is reached. Cross this and continue straight ahead to reach another wall boundary with Pendle Way witch waymarkers. Turn left and follow the wall to a ladder stile. Cross this and drop down to the beck then up the other side to a telegraph pole and a waymarker post. Turn at right angles by the post and head back to a gate and stile. Go straight ahead across a boggy field and head directly for the nearby farmhouse.

③ Cross a stile in front of the farmhouse and keep to the left of it to join an access

The Walk

① Start on the road in front of the church and follow the track (Harden Road) which leads up the left hand side of the babbling beck – a road runs parallel to it on the other side and soon joins it from the right. Bear left and follow the lane uphill between houses and through a gate. A farm track is now followed leading to two gates. Go through the wooden gate on the right and continue along the field edge to cross a ladder stile in the wall. Continue in the same

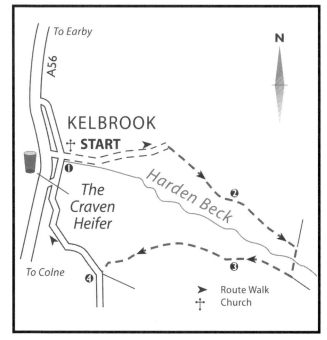

To Earby

A56

N

KELBROOK

✝ **START**

❶

The Craven Heifer

Harden Beck

❷

To Colne **❹**

❸

➤ Route Walk
✝ Church

The parish church with four clock faces

track which leads to the farm. This track is now followed for nearly a mile and winds around the hillside offering a good view which includes the mill town of Earby (to your right) and Blacko Tower. The track eventually meets a lane.

④ Turn right along the lane and this is now followed for the next ½ mile back to Kelbrook. At the crossroads turn right and this leads onto the main village street. At the church turn left to reach the A56. Cross this with great care to visit the pub.

PLACES OF INTEREST NEARBY

A few miles north of Kelbrook along the A56 is the **Yorkshire Dales Lead Mining Museum** at **Earby** (telephone: 01282 841422). This is signposted right off the A road. The museum is housed in an old grammar school complete with historic water wheel and contains unique exhibits charting the history of the local mining industry. Just to the south of Kelbrook along the A56 is **Foulridge Wharf** where canal boats along the Leeds-Liverpool Canal can be viewed or you can even take a cruise in one of them, heading for the Pennines or to Burnley. There is a tearoom and picnic area here as well as informal walks along the nearby Foulridge Reservoirs.

Chipping
The Tillotsons Arms

MAP: OUTDOOR LEISURE 41 FOREST OF BOWLAND (GR 623433)

WALK 13

DISTANCE: $3\frac{1}{4}$ MILES

DIRECTIONS TO START: THE VILLAGE IS 4 MILES NORTH OF LONGRIDGE ALONG MINOR LANES. FOLLOW THE ROAD SIGNS FROM LONGRIDGE WHICH IS SITUATED AT THE JUNCTION OF THE B6243 AND B5269.
PARKING: FREE CAR PARK NEAR THE CHURCH AND BEHIND THE COBBLED CORNER CAFÉ.

Chipping is a well-known village, much frequented by weekend visitors who stroll around the winding lanes of 17th century houses, visit the medieval church or sample the pubs. Situated on the banks of a brook, it nestles in the lush pastoral countryside of the Hodder Valley, in the shadows of the Bowland hills to the north and wooded Longridge Fell to the south. In medieval times it was a market centre for the surrounding rural area but in the 18th and 19th century water-powered mills along Chipping Brook sprang up and the village's heritage of craft industries can still be seen today in the chair works.

This walk heads north from the village along a quiet lane and field paths. It then follows back roads on the edge of the Bowland hills and returns to Chipping through lush pastures. There are views north to the spur of Parlick and south to Longridge Fell.

The Tillotsons Arms

Taking its name from a prominent local family, the Tillotsons Arms is sandwiched within a row of some of Chipping's most historic buildings. Next to the pub is the house and shop – one of the oldest post offices in the locality – which were built in 1668 by the London merchant John Brabin. The Tillotsons Arms remains a friendly locals' pub with quality food available at lunchtimes and in the evenings every day (note that it is closed on Monday afternoon from 3 pm until 5 pm). This Whitbread house serves cask ales including Flowers IPA. Telephone: 01995 61568.

The Walk

① From the car park face the church and turn left along the lane signed as Church Rake. Follow it past houses and when it forks bear right, continuing uphill then past a Chair Works. Opposite the mill pond leave the lane on the right by crossing a stile alongside a gate to Austin House.

② Follow the footpath uphill. Cross another stile and when the path forks into two at a waymarker post in the

PLACES OF INTEREST NEARBY

Just outside the village is the **Bowland Wild Boar Park** (telephone: 01995 615554). This is a fascinating outdoor venue, allowing all the family to see wild boars, llamas, wallabies, red squirrels and other animals and for children to feed the springtime lambs. There is also a café on site and plenty of woodland walks.

middle of a field, bear left to reach woodland. Go over a stile and bear left through the trees to cross a footbridge. Turn right and head uphill to a stone cottage. Join the track to the left of the cottage and turn left along it. Follow the track until it meets a minor lane at a gate.

③ Turn left along the lane and follow it gradually downhill until it reaches the junction with another minor lane on the right. Turn right along this adjoining lane and it meanders downhill to a wooded valley then uphill to reach another lane junction. Go straight ahead at this junction, following the lane uphill for a further $\frac{1}{4}$ mile until it meets a lane on the right running down from the moorland spur of Parlick.

④ Leave the road here on the left along a signed path opposite the junction. Cross the stile and follow the wall side downhill to cross another stile. Go directly ahead from here and cross a stream in the field corner. Follow the field edge alongside the

A lonely road to Parlick hill

stream towards a barn. Just before the barn, cross steps over the stream to reach another stile.

⑤ Cross this wall stile and go directly ahead, crossing two more stiles to join a farm drive. Turn left along this and follow it down to a lane. Turn right along the lane and it is now followed all the way back to the village car park.

Waddington
The Lower Buck Inn

MAP: OUTDOOR LEISURE 41 FOREST OF BOWLAND (GR 728438)

WALK 14

DISTANCE: $3\frac{1}{4}$ MILES

DIRECTIONS TO START: JOIN THE B6478 IN CLITHEROE TOWN CENTRE AND FOLLOW THE SIGNS FOR SLAIDBURN. WADDINGTON VILLAGE IS JUST 1 MILE NORTH OF CLITHEROE.
PARKING: ROADSIDE PARKING ON THE LANE BY THE PARISH CHURCH.

When the River Ribble formed the county boundary between Lancashire and Yorkshire hereabouts, Waddington was just a mile into Yorkshire. Not surprising then that its past history is embroiled with the War of the Roses as the defeated Henry VI stayed at Waddington Hall in 1464 before being captured by the Yorkists along the Ribble. Like Newton to the north, Waddington was also linked with the Parker family of nearby Browsholme Hall as Robert Parker founded the village almshouses for the widows of the parish. Handloom weavers also worked in the cottages and the pretty brook which runs through the centre of the village once supported local industries like a cotton spinning mill.

This walk follows the field paths west and north of Waddington before returning to the village past the old almshouses and village pump erected in 1700.

The Lower Buck Inn

This delightful country inn is now distinguished from the other Buck Inn in the village by the prefix of 'Lower'. The preponderance of Buck Inns hereabouts (see also the pub visited in Walk 11) is a clear indication that we are in the ancient hunting Forest of Bowland and the sign over the front entrance is another reminder of this. The Lower Buck is a large, rambling, stone-walled inn which overlooks a cobbled courtyard and is understandably preserved as a Grade I listed building. Very welcoming to families, the inn has a beer garden and restaurant as well as accommodation. This free house offers a wide selection of cask ales including Theakston Best Bitter and Burton Ale. Telephone: 01200 28705.

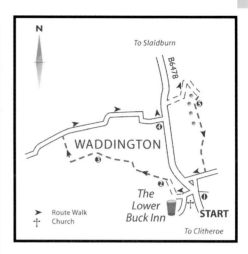

The Walk

① Start by the parish church near the centre of the village and walk along the lane past the church towards the Lower Buck Inn. Continue straight ahead behind the pub to reach the driveway entrance to The Roost. Do not go up the driveway but turn sharp right by the gate and follow a hedge side. At the end of the drive by a cottage go through a white gate and cross a stream at a stone bridge. Cross a step stile and continue straight ahead with the stream on your right.

② Enter a large field and go directly across the middle of it. On the opposite side of the field, cross a stile and follow a hedge side. Go through a gate and continue in the same direction to trees on the far side of the next field and cross a stile in the wooden fence. Turn right and join a track. Follow the track as it swings left and goes through a gate. Follow the fence side, crossing a stile into the next field, and continue along the field edge before bearing left away from the hedge at the opposite side of the field to cross a footbridge.

③ Continue straight ahead across the field to a stile. Cross this and follow the track in the same direction for a very short distance. Just before the track kinks left, cross a stile on the right. Bear right across this field and walk parallel to the fence line and farmhouse on your right. This leads to a stile into trees. On the far side of the woodland, cross a footbridge and reach a lane. Turn right along the lane. This is now followed for about $1/2$ mile until a road junction is reached.

④ Turn left and follow the road uphill until you reach the first house on the right hand side. Turn right off the road onto the footpath in front of the house, following

Field path to Waddington village

the access track to Feazer Farm. The track swings left and right through woodland. When it swings left towards buildings turn sharp right by a field gate and cross a stone stile at a wall corner on the left.

⑤ Follow the field edge overlooking the woodland to reach a stile and gate. Continue along the field edge in the next field and cross another stile, then continue downhill with the village over to your right. The path runs between two walls which form the access to the field and crosses a stile to reach a lane. Turn right here and follow the lane back into the village. At the road junction in the centre of the village turn left and walk alongside the stream to return to the parish church.

PLACES OF INTEREST NEARBY

The history of Bowland Forest's chief family, the Parkers, can be traced at their ancestral home of **Browsholme Hall** (telephone: 01254 826719). The Tudor and Elizabethan Hall is a fine example of a country mansion with numerous antiquities and collections to browse over. It is situated north of Bashall Eaves, just a few miles west of Waddington.

Inglewhite
The Green Man

<table>
<tr><td>**MAP:** EXPLORER 286 BLACKPOOL & PRESTON AND OUTDOOR LEISURE 41 FOREST OF BOWLAND (GR 547399)</td><td>**WALK 15**</td><td>**DISTANCE:** $3^3/_4$ MILES</td></tr>
</table>

DIRECTIONS TO START: THE VILLAGE IS SITUATED AT A CROSSROADS OF MINOR LANES $2^1/_2$ MILES EAST OF BILSBORROW ON THE A6. **PARKING:** PARK IN THE LAYBY (ON SILK MILL LANE) OPPOSITE THE PUB.

Bull-baiting, sheep selling, and horse trotting are just a few of the activities to have taken place on Inglewhite's large village green in bygone days. Though little more than a hamlet at a crossroads of rural lanes, Inglewhite's tall market cross – with a 1675 date stone – was the focal point for annual cattle fairs and drew rural folk in from the surrounding hills to barter, gamble and booze. The traditional inn and the adjacent green still pull in passing travellers whilst street names like Button Street and Silk Mill Lane are a lingering reminder of the hamlet's local textile industry.

This is an easy stroll through the lanes and hedged fields of pastoral country, though there are several stiles to climb. However, you are rewarded with plenty of views east to the moors and west to the Fylde plain.

The Green Man

Dating from 1809, the Green Man stands sentinel by the village crossroads and has become a tourist attraction in its own right. The traffic stops here at the welcoming inn which offers a large and varied menu of bar meals making use of local produce. Sandwiches, salads and vegetarian meals combine with hearty dishes such as steaks, mushroom and ale pie, steak and ale pie and lamb shanks as well as specials including mussels and tropical gammon. Then there are the traditional Sunday roasts as well as fresh salmon which ensure the inn is always popular at the weekends. Beers include John Smith's and Marston's Pedigree. Add to this mix the cosy lounge and wintertime log fire, the pool table and the beer garden and you may not want to leave. You may not need to – as there is a caravan and camp site at the rear of the inn. Food is served at lunchtimes and in the evenings every day. Telephone: 01995 640292.

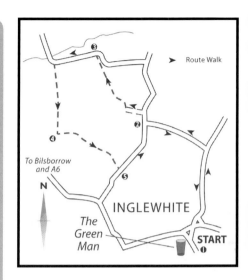

The Walk

① By the memorial on the green cross over to join Button Street which is signposted for Whitechapel and Oakenclough. The lane leads past cottages and after nearly ¹/₂ mile starts to bear right by a disused barn. Turn left here down the lane past Fairhurst Cottage. The lane drops gradually downhill to a T-junction.

② Turn right and then first left to join a footpath following a track towards cottages. Next to the driveway entrance to Wincroft Lodge cross a waymarked stile on the right. Follow the field edge path, keeping the garden boundary of the house on the left. Cross another stile at the next field boundary and continue in the same direction, keeping the hedge boundary immediately to the right. Further stiles lead to the bend of a minor lane.

③ Turn left along the lane which drops gradually downhill towards the wooded valley of the River Brock (a tributary of the River Wyre). Before a bridge over the river is reached, two footpath signs will be seen on the left. Take the upper of the two paths, crossing a stile and heading uphill across the middle of the field. Aim for a stile in the tree-lined hedge ahead. Two stiles lead across a hedged ditch and into a large field. Continue in the same direction with views right to the M6 and the Fylde. Over the rise of the hill, aim for a stone barn which is reached through a gate.

④ Keep the barn on the left and follow a hedged track for a short distance until it

The village green and war memorial

bends sharp right. Turn sharp left here and go through a gate. Almost immediately on the right cross two stiles and swing left down the bank of a wooded valley to reach a wooden footbridge. Cross this, then bear left to climb out of the valley and cross another stile. Follow the field edge and further stiles lead to a ladder stile by a farmyard barn. Cross this and turn left to join a lane.

⑤ Turn left along the lane and follow it for ¹/₄ mile until it reaches another lane on the right. This is the lane walked down

PLACES OF INTEREST NEARBY

Go north-east of Inglewhite to reach **Beacon Fell Country Park** (telephone: 01995 640557) which is worth visiting for the commanding views it offers across Bowland and Lancashire. There is a popular visitor centre here and a café as well as lots of opportunities for forest walks.

earlier. Turn right and retrace your steps, turning right at the top of the lane to return along the road leading to the village.

Pendleton
The Swan with Two Necks

| MAP: OUTDOOR LEISURE 41 FOREST OF BOWLAND (GR 755396) | WALK 16 | DISTANCE: 4 MILES |

DIRECTIONS TO START: PENDLETON IS 1$\frac{1}{2}$ MILES SOUTH-EAST OF CLITHEROE AND SITUATED TO THE EAST OF THE A59. THE PUB IS ON THE MAIN STREET IN THE CENTRE OF THE VILLAGE. **PARKING:** THERE IS A FREE PUBLIC CAR PARK ADJACENT TO THE SWAN WITH TWO NECKS.

The eyes of passing motorists on the busy A59 are drawn towards the brooding mass of Pendle Hill. But for those who only explore the delights of wild Pendle from this fast stretch of road around Clitheroe, ancient villages like Pendleton (the farmstead by the hill) will remain forever hidden from view. This linear Anglo-Saxon settlement – recorded in the Domesday Book – is only a stone's throw from the main highway. But it is easily missed. It is so well preserved that even the Victorian church and school at the top end of the village are relatively 'new'. Today the village cannot boast a shop yet little more than 50 years ago the village even had a police station!

This walk mixes lush pastures with the wild country on the lower slopes of Pendle Hill. It passes Pendleton Hall, once the home of the de Hoghton family, then climbs to rough moorland before following the lane up towards the Nick of Pendle, a popular viewpoint. It returns to the village through hedged fields and offers spectacular views across the rural Ribble Valley.

The Swan with Two Necks

The Swan with Two Necks is an interesting pub name usually accompanied by an inn sign with two swans. But the history of this inn name actually derives from the 'Swan with Two Nicks' which refers to two 'nicks' or marks on the beak of a swan to identify that they were the property of innkeepers rather than royalty so they could, in fact, be eaten without permission of the monarch! There are currently no signs of swans being kept outside the 1776 inn today but the friendly hostelry is diverting enough to linger awhile just in case swans come back and settle on the roadside beck. The street patio tables are very popular when the sun shines and there is a small beer garden at the rear of the pub. The Swan is an integral part of the local community since the inn doubles up as a post office branch – it opens up some mornings not to serve beer, but so the locals can get pensions and top up savings accounts! If you don't fancy buying a first class stamp then there is always Carslberg and Tetley's. Not to mention the quality home-cooked food available at lunchtimes and evenings every day of the week. Telephone: 01200 423112.

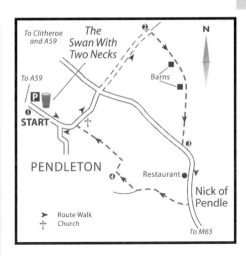

The Walk

① Walk up the main street alongside the stream and pass the old school and church. Continue along the road for about $1/2$ mile until it reaches a junction with another road. Cross this road and directly opposite go through a white gate along the access to Pendleton Hall. The access track bears left then right between farm buildings then goes through a gate. Continue straight ahead along the farm track with the views to the right taking in Pendle Hill. After about $1/2$ mile look out for a waymarker post indicating a footpath to the right. This is reached just before a gateway to some stone houses.

② Turn right and join this path. Cross a stile and head uphill towards a barn, keeping the stream and trees on your left. The path skirts around the left hand side of the barn and crosses a ladder stile in the wall corner. Keep walking straight ahead across boggy pasture and head in the direction of another barn. The path becomes vague but head for the barn and a footbridge below it is crossed. Bear left uphill from here and follow the wall side on the edge of the moor. Keep the wall on the right but when it turns at right angles bear slightly left along a faint path which heads to the road which will soon come into view ahead.

③ Turn left along the road and follow it uphill for about $1/4$ mile, passing the Wellsprings restaurant. Take care walking

A panorama of the Ribble Valley looking north to Bowland

along the road particularly where it bends sharply near the brow of the hill and at this point look for a stone stile indicating a path on the right hand side. Join this path and walk downhill to a gate in the wall on the left. Cross the stile and follow the track downhill with the lush parkland of the Ribble Valley below. Before farm buildings are reached cross a stone stile in the wall on the right. Follow this diagonally downhill to the farm where further stiles are crossed.

④ Walk straight ahead along a line of trees and telegraph poles and the path turns right over a stile and follows the next field edge to another stile. Cross this and turn left and there is a gentle descent through a large field leading to a gate and footbridge. Cross the stream, bear left and continue straight ahead with the stream on the left. This leads to a ford and you continue straight ahead to meet the village lane. Turn left and follow it back to the pub and car park.

PLACES OF INTEREST NEARBY
The historic market town of **Clitheroe** is just across the A59 and is a well-preserved Norman castle town with a museum and popular market. Rich in heritage, it also offers traditional shops, pubs and places to eat (Clitheroe tourist information centre, telephone: 01200 425566).

Roughlee
The Bay Horse Inn

MAP: OUTDOOR LEISURE 41 FOREST OF BOWLAND (GR 844404)

WALK 17

DISTANCE: 4 MILES

DIRECTIONS TO START: THE VILLAGE IS LOCATED ON THE CROSSROADS OF A MINOR LANE 1¼ MILES NORTH-WEST OF THE A682 AT BARROWFORD. **PARKING:** THERE IS LIMITED PARKING ALONGSIDE THE ROADSIDE STREAM ON EITHER SIDE OF THE BAY HORSE INN.

'Lancashire Witch Country' is the haunting name conjured up for the villages below the Big End of Pendle Hill. Roughlee, Barley and Newchurch are the central focus of this mysterious tract of medieval Pendle Forest which has a well-recorded history of 17th century witchcraft. The Lancashire Witch Trials of the 1600s were very much a real event and one of Roughlee's wealthy residents – Alice Nutter of Roughlee Old Hall – was hanged at Lancaster Castle after being found guilty of being a witch.

The spirit of the witches pervades this route as for part of the way we follow the Pendle Way footpath with its distinctive witch waymarkers. We climb out of the village and walk on field paths along a ridge before taking quiet lanes and woodland tracks to Barley village at the foot of Pendle Hill. The Pendle Way is then followed back to Roughlee, with the stream that links the two villages close at hand.

The Bay Horse Inn

This stone inn, once a farmhouse, overlooks the crossroads and dominates the tiny village which once had a large mill on the stream as its main focus. The Bay Horse is a traditional country pub which offers excellent tasty bar meals as well as à la carte dining in the restaurant. A play area is also provided for children and there is a beer garden. The popular Sunday carvery is served all day until 8 pm and meals are available at lunchtimes and in the evenings on all other days of the week. Beers on offer at the Bay Horse include Greene King, Ruddles Best, Old Speckled Hen and Theakston Best. Telephone: 01282 613683.

The Walk

① From the pub cross the road bridge along the road signed for Barrowford. Climb uphill and when the road bends sharp left take the paved footpath straight ahead. This immediately turns sharp left, crosses a drive and goes over a stile to follow a field edge path alongside a wall. Cross the stile on the opposite side of the field to join a farm lane. Turn right here and when it forks bear right over the cattle grid to follow a farm track. This soon reaches two gateways. Go through the right gateway and continue with the wall side on the immediate left. The path follows a raised bank and leads to a roadside cottage which is a pleasantly placed refreshment stop.

② Turn right and follow the road steeply downhill to the valley with a view of

PLACES OF INTEREST NEARBY

Only a mile or so away from the village is the **Pendle Heritage Centre** in **Barrowford** (telephone: 01282 695366). Housed in a 17th century farmhouse, this offers an insight into the history and heritage of Pendle country. It includes farming displays, a café, a shop, a toll house and gardens. The farmhouse itself, Park Hill, was once the home of the Bannister family whose descendants included athlete Roger Bannister, the first man to break the 4 minute mile! The centre is located at the junction of the A682 and B6247 in the heart of Barrowford.

Blacko Tower over to the right. At the minor crossroads continue straight ahead along the lane signposted for Barley. After passing Thorneyholme Hall the road starts to climb again and just before a phone box is reached join an unsigned track on the left hand side of the road. This walled track climbs uphill and enters woodland. The view to Pendle Hill opens up ahead after you emerge from the trees and the stony track leads all the way to Barley village.

③ When the track meets a road, turn right and at the next road junction by the village hall turn right again and follow the pavement past the small visitor centre, picnic area and toilets. After the car park, turn left at the next access by a gate and follow the signed bridleway which leads into a cobbled courtyard of pretty cottages. Go straight ahead through a gate and follow the pleasant stream side path for about $1/4$ mile until you reach an access lane to stone cottages on your left just before a bridge over the stream is reached.

④ Turn left up the lane which starts to

Roadside refreshments

climb gradually. Halfway up the hill between houses look out for a tiny red-brick building on the right and leave the road here along the path waymarked with

the distinctive witch waymarkers of the Pendle Way footpath. Keep following this signed route and the path leads through shady woodland. Ignore the first stile reached on the right but continue uphill to further stiles and follow the fence line as the path drops down to a driveway. Turn left along the drive and a quiet lane is reached.

⑤ Turn right here and the lane is followed for the next $1/2$ mile back to Roughlee. After the caravan park is passed look out for a signed footpath by a gap in the wall on the right. This drops down steps and is a shortcut leading back to the pub.

Goosnargh
The Grapes Inn

MAP: EXPLORER 286 BLACKPOOL & PRESTON (GR 559368)	WALK 18	DISTANCE: 2½ MILES

DIRECTIONS TO START: LEAVE THE A6 AT THE BROUGHTON CROSSROADS AND HEAD EAST ALONG THE B5269 TOWARDS LONGRIDGE. TURN LEFT INTO GOOSNARGH AND BEAR RIGHT AT THE FAR END OF THE VILLAGE GREEN TO REACH THE CHURCH AND PUBS. **PARKING:** IN FRONT OF THE CHURCH OR ALONG THE ADJACENT LANE.

Goosnargh, pronounced 'Gooz-na', is deep in farming country. It takes its name from the 'goose field' which forms the unusually large village green and in bygone days curious Prestonians flocked here at Easter and Whitsun to enjoy traditional country fairs and sample the local delicacy of Goosnargh cakes. The townsfolk obviously liked this slice of rural life and the village's location has made it one of Preston's main commuter villages. Suburban houses have sprung up along the south side of the green but reminders of the old village remain in the parish church, the ancient inns, Bushell House which was built in 1720 as a rest home and 13th century Chingle Hall. Not to mention the goose green itself and the old hostelries that surround it.

This is an easy stroll crossing the fields that encircle the village. There are several stiles to negotiate and the walk passes historic Chingle Hall before returning to the village green.

The Grapes Inn

The Grapes is certainly one of the oldest inns in this book and, in fact, one of the oldest inns in Lancashire. It was even an inn at the time of the Domesday Book and in its early days was known as the 'Saracen's Head' – a common pub name at the time of the Crusades – and later as the 'General Elliot'. As the former village coaching inn it retains an old-fashioned country interior and an ivy clad exterior. Bar meals and restaurant meals are available and as befits the village of the 'goose green' why not try the speciality Goosnargh Duckling or the succulent Ribble Valley Roast Shoulder of Lamb and wash it all down with the Black Sheep Bitter? Food is available all day on Sundays and at lunchtimes and in the evenings on other days except Mondays – there is no food on Mondays except for bank holidays. Telephone: 01772 865234.

The Walk

① In front of the Grapes Inn walk along the lane, passing the imposing Bushell House on the left. When the lane soon turns sharp left go straight ahead along a track then almost immediately sharp right up the drive to Bushell's Cottage. Keep the white metal fence immediately to the right and cross a wooden stile at the rear of the garden. Turn left and walk straight ahead across a large field to a stile at the opposite end. Cross this and follow a narrow path to a road.

② Turn right along the pavement and follow it until the hospital entrance gates are reached on the opposite side of the road. Go through the gates and up the tree-lined drive which is signed for Whittingham and Goosnargh Sports and Social Club. When the driveway bends left around the wall of a new house, turn right and follow the footpath alongside the wall which leads to a stile.

③ Cross this and turn left to follow the field edge alongside the buildings of Whittingham Hall until a gate and stile are reached by a farmyard access. Do not cross the stile but turn right by the gate and follow the hedge side of the same large field to reach further stiles. Cross these and turn left to cross another stile into an adjoining field. Turn right here, now walking with the hedge on the right. This skirts the fence of a deer enclosure and reaches a metal farm gate. Go through the gate and down the driveway past Chingle Hall to meet a road.

④ Turn right on the road and after approximately 60 yards turn left up a footpath on the opposite side. Cross a stile and follow the hedge side to a gap

The parish church

PLACES OF INTEREST NEARBY

The **National Football Museum** (telephone: 01772 908442) is located at Preston North End's Deepdale football stadium at nearby Preston. You don't need to be a footie fanatic to enjoy the interesting range of exhibits which include the Stanley Matthews collection and the legendary crossbar from the 1966 Wembley World Cup Final. But if you are, then you can indulge yourself by reliving all your favourite moments in football history.

and continue in the same direction in the next field with the hedge now on the right. Cross a metal stile by a gate then immediately cross a stile on the right into a field. Skirt around a pond behind which is another hidden stile. Cross this and follow a narrow path behind gardens to reach a road. Continue straight ahead past the houses to the village green and turn left at the road junction to reach the church and pubs.

Ribchester
The White Bull

DIRECTIONS TO START: THE VILLAGE IS SITUATED ALONG THE B6245 BETWEEN BLACKBURN AND LONGRIDGE. **PARKING:** THE PAY AND DISPLAY CAR PARK (ALLOW ENOUGH TIME FOR THE WALK, PUB AND MUSEUM VISIT) IS THE FIRST RIGHT TURN AFTER PASSING THE BLACK BULL ON CHURCH STREET. IT OVERLOOKS A PLAYGROUND.

Ribchester is one of Lancashire's most famous villages, dating back to Roman times. It even has a Latin name – Bremetennacum. For Governor Agricola built a fort here in AD 79 to guard a crossing point on the River Ribble. Stone and pillars from the fort are thought to have been used in the construction of the village church which is well worth a visit. The low-lying settlement is prone to flooding whilst the plain provides some of the lushest cattle pastures in the whole of the county.

The walk is a very gentle saunter over the stiles and fields surrounding the village. It also takes in a spectacular view of the Ribble Valley and passes the remains of a Roman bath house.

The White Bull

This imposing hostelry fits in well with the surrounding 17th and 18th century cottages. Though the present building has a 1707 date stone it is much older. It was once the local court house and the pillars at the front porch are Roman in origin as are the inn's cellars which are believed to be on the site of a Roman temple. Today, this popular sprawling hostelry provides tempting fare for hungry wayfarers including speciality White Bull Lamb Busters, White Bull Cold Platters, a good vegetarian menu and weekly specials. Beers available are Tetley Smooth, Boddingtons Cask and Smooth and Black Sheep Bitter. Families are welcome and the inn has a walled garden, a restaurant, a games room and offers accommodation. Food is available at lunchtimes and in the evenings on Monday to Saturday and from 12 noon until 10.30 pm on Sundays. As you sit enjoying yourself, reflect on the fact you are at the very heart of Roman Lancashire – and troops marched across the Ribble here en route for the wild Scottish borders. No Lamb Busters for them! Telephone: 01254 878303.

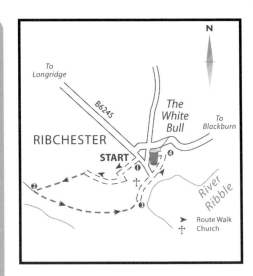

The Walk

① Turn right out of the car park and follow the bridleway straight ahead along a private road. At a cattle grid, take the right fork and follow the lane signed for Parsonage Farm Cottage. Go over another cattle grid and as the lane bends around to some trees look out for a stile and a gate on the left. Join this path and head for a line of electricity pylons. The path leads to a gate in a hedge. Turn left and keep the hedge side on the right to cross under the pylons. Further stiles along the hedge side are crossed before a field overlooking the river is reached.

② Go straight across this field to a stile by a gate but do not cross it. Instead, turn sharp left and follow the fence line of the same field back to a wooden gate. This is a bridleway and the river is to the immediate right of the fence. Go through the kissing gate and join a farm track leading past Boat House Barn. The track heads back towards the village and after about ¹/₂ mile farm buildings are reached.

③ Go straight on here and the track bears slightly left and joins the road. Pass the Museum and Rectory and alongside the primary school join the riverside path signed as the Ribble Way. There is a panoramic view upstream here towards lofty Pendle Hill. Follow the path under

Looking upstream along the River Ribble

trees and alongside a stream until steps leading up to the Roman bath house are quickly reached on the left. Information panels shed light on the history of this site.

④ Go out through the opposite access point and at the adjoining lane turn left. Go left again at the next lane and walk down to the White Bull. To complete the walk from here walk along the adjoining lane to the left of the White Bull car park and then turn first left to reach the playing field car park.

PLACES OF INTEREST NEARBY

You do not have to go far to extend your day out in the Ribble Valley. Ribchester's very own **Roman Museum** (telephone: 01254 878261) is passed on the walk and occupies part of the site of the old fort. Many relics found in the vicinity, including coins and pottery, are on display here. A short drive away, along the A59 towards Clitheroe, the historic Ribble Valley town of **Whalley** is similarly rich in history. English Heritage maintain the 14th century **Whalley Abbey** (telephone: 01254 822268) which is open to visitors.

Longton
The Dolphin Inn

DIRECTIONS TO START: LONGTON IS SITUATED WEST OFF THE A59 BYPASS BETWEEN MUCH HOOLE AND HUTTON. **PARKING:** THERE IS AMPLE PARKING AT THE LONGTON BRICKCROFT NATURE RESERVE WHICH IS OFF LIVERPOOL ROAD ON THE SOUTH SIDE OF THE VILLAGE (GR 479251). ALTERNATIVELY, THE WALK CAN BE STARTED AT THE DOLPHIN INN AT THE END OF MARSH LANE TO THE WEST OF THE VILLAGE. THERE IS LIMITED PARKING ON THE ROAD OUTSIDE THE PUB (GR 459254).

Longton is a large dormitory village which has become a very desirable place to live for commuters to Preston. But with the wild salty marshes of the Ribble Estuary close at hand, the village has retained its country roots. Behind the new residential estates you are never far away from the traditional patchwork of hedges, fields and rural lanes. Longton once boasted its own train station and brick works – the site of the latter having been reclaimed as a popular bird-rich nature reserve.

The reserve is an ideal start/finish point for a walk which heads seawards and includes a bracing stroll along the flood bank of the Ribble Estuary with far-reaching views over to the Fylde coast. The Dolphin Inn is a welcome halfway stopping point before a quiet country lane is followed back to the village.

The Dolphin Inn

The Dolphin is known locally as the 'Flying Fish', and is an unassuming red-brick cottage. Popular with the locals who know it exists and can find it, it is also well known to ramblers as it has the odd distinction of being the official starting point of a long-distance footpath – the Ribble Way. The Dolphin is literally perched at the end of the road – and from here there is nothing but the tidal marsh and estuary of the River Ribble. The Ribble Way leaves here and heads inland (eventually) for a further 73 miles to its source in the Yorkshire Dales. Just think about that journey as you sit back and relax over a glass of Thwaites Bitter or Best Mild in this hidden gem which, understandably, can provide you with a plate of hearty fish and chips or a hot meaty pie to warm you up just in case there's a brisk wind blowing off the marsh. Food is served daily and there is also a beer garden and children's play area. Telephone: 01772 612032.

The Walk

① Go out through the main entrance to the reserve by the visitor centre and cross the road with care to join Hall Lane alongside a bakery. The lane is followed straight ahead for the next $^3/_4$ mile and it soon passes the houses and becomes a stone track and a grass path between hedges before reaching a gate by a farm. Go through the farmyard and turn left onto the adjoining lane. After a very short distance the lane starts to bend left by some electricity pylons. Leave it at this point via a field gate on the right.

② Cross the field along the raised bank and beyond it continue in the same direction keeping the fence line of the adjacent field on your right. Follow the fence line back to another raised bank and follow this to a footbridge and stile. Go straight ahead along the high flood bank from the stile until another stile is reached after about $^1/_4$ mile. To visit the Dolphin Inn at this point, turn right and cross the stile and follow the lane for about 250 yards. Retrace your steps back to the flood bank to continue the walk.

③ Continue along the flood bank with views looking across the estuary and when the bank forks into two, bear right to stiles. Cross the stile and footbridge to the right of a gate and follow the field edge to a farm access road. Turn right and follow this down to an adjoining lane (Marsh Lane). Turn left and follow this only for a short distance until Back Lane is reached on the left. Turn up this and it soon becomes a rough country track enclosed by hedges. Follow it for about $^1/_2$ mile until a new residential estate is reached. By greenhouses on the left, turn right along a public bridleway enclosed by gardens. This leads to the main road through the village.

PLACES OF INTEREST NEARBY
The visitor centre at the **Longton Brickcroft Nature Reserve** (telephone: 01772 611497) provides information on local walks and wildlife. Take advantage of the proximity of **Preston** – which now has city status! – to visit some of its attractions which include the **Harris Museum and Art Gallery** (telephone: 01772 258248).

The Ribble Way across lonely Longton Marsh

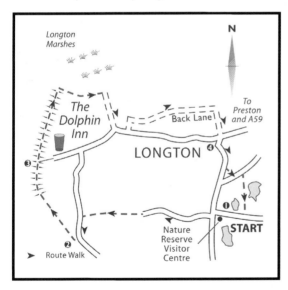

④ Take care and cross over, continuing straight ahead past the hardware shop along the pavement. After a short distance, bear left through a metal kissing gate and follow a tarmac footpath through a small park. Follow the path through trees on the far side of the park and cross the estate road to a kissing gate which leads back into the nature reserve. Follow the path with the lake on the left and cross a minor lane via kissing gates then turn right and skirt around the next lake to reach the car park.

Pleasington
The Butlers Arms

MAP: EXPLORER 287 WEST PENNINE MOORS (GR 643265)

WALK 21

DISTANCE: 2½ MILES

DIRECTIONS TO START: PLEASINGTON IS SITUATED ON A MINOR ROAD EAST OF BLACKBURN. IT IS ½ MILE NORTH OF FENISCOWLES ON THE A674. THE VILLAGE ALSO HAS A TRAIN STATION ON THE PRESTON–BLACKBURN LINE. **PARKING:** THERE IS ROADSIDE PARKING IN THE CENTRE OF THE VILLAGE CLOSE TO THE BUTLERS ARMS.

Pleasington is a historic township that has become an attractive commuter village protected from the urban encroachment of neighbouring Blackburn by the lofty countryside of Witton Country Park. Hilly cattle pastures predominate in this surprisingly attractive rural stretch of the River Darwen which rises in the West Pennine Moors and flows north-westwards to join the River Ribble. The Catholic Priory, built in 1819 in a flamboyant medieval style, is also a local landmark passed on this walk.

The route begins and ends at the pub and includes some steep ascents through the hilly pastures on the west side of the Darwen Valley. There are extensive views, particularly southwards, and the walk drops down to the River Darwen before climbing back up to the village.

The Butlers Arms

This roadside pub in the heart of the village takes its name from the local squire, John Butler, who built the nearby Priory in 1819. The extensive network of footpaths hereabouts makes this attractive hostelry popular with midweek and weekend ramblers. Walkers are made very welcome and the homely interior is a perfect resting place in which to choose from the extensive menu or sample real ales including rare bitters like Black Cat and Barngate Cracker. Food is available at lunchtimes and in the evenings all week and from 12 noon until 5 pm on Sundays. There is a children's menu, a play area and a beer garden. Telephone: 01254 201561.

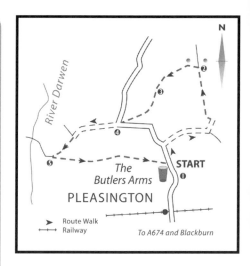

The Walk

① Walk along the main village street, passing the Priory on your right, then turn immediately right up Old Hall Lane. Keep to the lane until the last house is reached, then turn left to a gate and stile. Cross the stile and walk straight ahead up a sunken lane. The path climbs uphill through a very large field. Head straight up through the middle of the field towards three large trees and a line of telegraph poles. Beyond the trees keep going straight uphill until eventually a gate and a stile in the stone wall near the top right hand corner of the field are reached. Take a breather here and enjoy the view looking back downhill.

② Cross the stile and enter the silver birch woodland. Almost immediately turn left and leave the main track, instead following a very faint path through the woodland and over the brow of a hill to reach a waymarked stile at the edge of a field. This is easy to miss as it cannot be seen until it is almost reached. Cross this stile and follow the field edge to reach a gate to the left of farm buildings.

③ Do not follow the track swinging right to the farm but go through a narrow swing gate on the left leading into an adjoining field. Walk downhill and bear right to go through an access into the next field. Continue straight ahead through a series of boggy fields heading towards trees and soon following the upper edge of a large field sloping steeply downhill. Cross a stile in a fence and walk straight ahead to the opposite corner of this field where a stile leads onto a narrow path which leads to a road.

④ Cross the road and by the phone box walk down Long Lane. This becomes a stone track which drops downhill offering a fine view of the wooded cliff on the opposite side of the valley. At the junction of tracks go through the gateway to

Pleasington Priory

Higher Park Farm and then go through another gateway to the right of the farm buildings and the path continues downhill as a muddy track. Head for a wall in the valley bottom and look for the kink in the wall where there is a hidden stile.

⑤ Cross this stile and follow the path with the wall on the left. Cross the next stile and follow a field edge path which soon climbs uphill. Near the top of the hill the path bears right and crosses another stile to join a track by a thatch roofed house. Go straight ahead along a residential cul-de-sac to reach the main village street alongside the pub.

PLACES OF INTEREST NEARBY

Just to the east of the village is **Witton Country Park** which has picnic sites, nature trails, a visitor centre and tearoom (telephone: 01254 55423). Venture slightly further east from here to visit **Blackburn** which has a town centre museum and art gallery (telephone: 01254 667130) housing Japanese prints and cultural collections.

Riley Green
The Royal Oak Hotel

| **MAP:** EXPLORER 287 WEST PENNINE MOORS (GR 622255) | WALK 22 | **DISTANCE:** 3¼ MILES |

DIRECTIONS TO START: THE VILLAGE IS SITUATED AT THE JUNCTION OF THE A6061 AND THE A675 WEST OF BLACKBURN, ¾ MILE NORTH OF JUNCTION 3 OF THE M65. **PARKING:** VERY LIMITED APART FROM THE ROYAL OAK CAR PARKS FOR PATRONS.

Riley Green is a hamlet straggling a main road in the hillside shadow of Hoghton Tower, one of the county's most famous stately homes. Kings were no strangers to staunchly royalist rural Lancashire and in 1617 the de Hoghton family entertained King James I, offering him the finest cut of beef reared on the rolling pastures of the Darwen Valley. Such loyalty to the King proved costly as during the Civil War Hoghton Tower came under siege by the Roundheads and the mansion's tower was partly destroyed. Peace has since descended on Riley Green though the royalist connection lingers in the name of the roadside inn.

There are panoramic views for much of the length of this stroll which passes over the hill of the Tower and offers distant glimpses of both Preston and Blackburn – two sprawling urban townscapes separated by a rolling clump of surprisingly pleasant countryside.

The Royal Oak Hotel

In the 17th century James I famously knighted his loin of beef up the hill at Hoghton Tower. Little did he know that less than half a century later his grandson Prince Charles, later Charles II, was to famously hide in an oak tree to escape being caught by Cromwell's army during the English Civil War. When Charles II was restored to the throne in 1660 the 'Royal Oak' became justly celebrated and inns all over the country were named after the event which marked the saving of the monarchy. The inn sign at Riley Green depicts the event, hanging over the front of the long building which actually dates from the reign of James I. Inside the pub, the olde-worlde atmosphere remains with four low oak-beamed rooms served by a central bar. Log fires burn here in winter whilst in summer roadside tables and a pleasant little beer garden allow patrons to soak up the sun. Serving Thwaites Best, a local brew from Blackburn, the Royal Oak is a past award winner noted in CAMRA good beer guides.

A regular menu and daily blackboard specials provide hearty meals and food is served at lunchtimes and evenings every day. Well-behaved dogs on leads are also welcome. Telephone: 01254 201445.

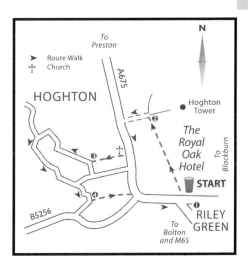

The Walk

① Walk up Green Lane between the Royal Oak and the cottages. Cross the ladder stile at the end of the lane and go straight ahead up the hill. Cross further stiles, to reach a gate and ladder stile with Hoghton Tower over to the right. There is a good view from here to Darwen Tower. Cross over the stile and go straight ahead through woodland to cross another stile and drop downhill to reach the driveway to Hoghton Tower.

② Turn left and follow the drive downhill to the road. Turn left and follow the pavement uphill past Hoghton church. Cross over the busy road, with care, to the church side. Immediately after the churchyard turn right and follow a footpath which leads up steps and runs along the church wall to a stile. Follow the field edge to a stile leading to cottages at the bend in the lane.

③ Bear right and follow the lane past the cottages. The lane climbs very gradually then drops downhill before swinging left to meet another road at the top of a hill, with a good view looking north to Preston. Follow the lane around past farms and at the next road junction continue straight ahead along Windmill Lane. When this

Looking south to Darwen Tower and the West Pennines

road starts to bend around to the right by a gate to an old barn, look out on the left hand side for two signed footpaths.

④ Take the nearest of the two paths, indicated by a signpost and stile by a tree. Cross the stile and follow a field edge path by a drain. Further stiles are crossed and the path then runs with the field boundary on the left. Cross another stile to reach the road by a junction. Cross over Sandy Lane at the junction then continue straight ahead along the pavement of the main road back to the Royal Oak. Cross carefully over the busy road to return to the start point.

PLACES OF INTEREST NEARBY

You don't need to travel far to visit one of this area's main tourist attractions. **Hoghton Tower** (telephone: 01254 852986) is passed along the walk and is the historic home of the de Hoghton family. Open to the public on certain days the house offers an insight into Tudor and Elizabethan manorial life and the guided tour takes you from the grand banqueting hall where King James I was entertained to the underground passages and cells.

Brindle
The Cavendish Arms

MAP: EXPLORER 286 BLACKPOOL & PRESTON AND EXPLORER 287 WEST PENNINE MOORS (GR. 599240)

WALK 23

DISTANCE: 2 MILES

DIRECTIONS TO START: THE VILLAGE IS SITUATED HALFWAY ALONG THE B5256 BETWEEN WHITTLE-LE-WOODS AND HOGHTON. START ALONG WATER LANE WHICH RUNS BETWEEN THE CHURCH AND THE CAVENDISH ARMS. **PARKING:** ROADSIDE PARKING ALONG WATER LANE BETWEEN THE CHURCH AND THE PRIMARY SCHOOL OR AT THE PUB ON THE MAIN STREET (PATRONS ONLY).

Brindle takes its name from the 'bryn', the spring – or several springs in fact – which rise here in the hollow of the hills. The village remains relatively unchanged since the Civil War when Roundheads and Cavaliers skirmished hereabouts. It is almost the perfect village – with church, school and inn in close proximity just up the hill from the preserved village 'pound' where cattle were collected from the surrounding pastures. The annual Brindle Races were a popular horse event through the village from top to bottom though it is hard to believe they attracted 20,000 spectators. The only intrusion to this rural scene now is the nearby M65. But even this doesn't spoil the views, which on clear days extend northwards to Bowland and the Lake District.

The walk is short and sweet. It starts on Water Lane by the primary school and is a very gentle stroll through farming country. Field paths and quiet hedged lanes are followed, but you may be surprised at the high proportion of stiles for a walk of such a short distance!

The Cavendish Arms

This large country inn dominates the village and takes its name from the lords of the manor. The Cavendish family bought the estate from an earlier lord, Thomas Garard, who actually lived in the building which is now the inn. Garard was forced to sell his Brindle estate to pay for his release from the Tower of London after he had supported the ill-fated Catholic Mary, Queen of Scots against young Elizabeth I. The present Cavendish Arms is a welcoming hostelry for patrons in search of fine food in pleasant surroundings and both bar meals and bistro meals are available at lunchtimes and in the evenings every day. Burtonwood Bitter is available as well as a changing guest bitter. Telephone: 01254 852912.

The Walk

① If you are parked at the pub, walk down adjoining Water Lane as far as the village primary school on the right hand side. On the far side of the school turn right and follow the footpath leading through two gates to a stile in a field. Bear left and walk past a pond to another stile. Cross this and turn left, walking uphill along the tree-lined field edge to cross a stile into the next field. There is a good view north and west from here towards Bowland and Preston. Continue in the same direction along the field edges and further stiles are crossed. Eventually, a final stile leads out on to a lane by a red telephone box.

② Turn left onto the lane and after a very

PLACES OF INTEREST NEARBY

In nearby Leyland there are two contrasting attractions. **Worden Park** (telephone: 01772 421109) is a historic town park with a maze, formal gardens and a miniature steam railway. The **British Commercial Vehicle Museum** (telephone: 01772 451011) celebrates the heritage of British Leyland and houses an interesting collection of vehicles from a bygone age – from horse-drawn carriages to motor buses.

short distance join the first footpath on the right which begins as a field access through three gates. Continue along the field edge until two stiles are reached by another gate. Do not go through the stile straight ahead but cross the stile on the left and walk diagonally across the next field to a stile near the opposite corner. There are two stiles here as well! Take the one on the left and cross into the next field, now walking with the field edge on the right. Cross a stile by a gate which leads to a lane junction.

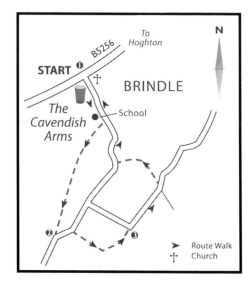

A patchwork of fields and hedges

③ Continue straight ahead in the same direction along the hedged lane. When the lane starts to kink left you will see footpath signs with stiles leading into fields on opposite sides of the lane. Cross the stile on the left. Follow the field edge to another stile and continue as the path drops downhill to yet another stile. Go straight ahead uphill in the next field and a further stile leads out onto a lane again. Turn right and the lane drops downhill and soon comes back to the school. Continue up to the junction with the village high street to reach the pub.

Haslingden Grane
The Duke of Wellington

<table>
<tr><td>MAP: EXPLORER 287 WEST PENNINE MOORS (GR 752232)</td><td>WALK 24</td><td>DISTANCE: 4 MILES</td></tr>
</table>

DIRECTIONS TO START: THE CLOUGH HEAD INFORMATION CENTRE AND PICNIC SITE IS SIGNED ON THE A6177 BETWEEN BLACKBURN AND HASLINGDEN. **PARKING:** THERE IS A LARGE CAR PARK AT THE CLOUGH HEAD INFORMATION CENTRE. THE CAR PARK IS LOCKED AT NIGHT SO CHECK CLOSING TIMES ON THE INFORMATION BOARD. ALTERNATIVELY, THE WALK CAN BE STARTED AT THE DUKE OF WELLINGTON (GR 767229), FURTHER EAST ALONG THE A6177, WHERE THERE IS A LARGE CAR PARK FOR PATRONS ONLY.

aslingden Grane survives on the map but you would be hard pushed to pinpoint an actual village by that name. It is a 'ghost' community. The valley which once housed many thriving farmers, weavers and whisky distillers has been largely deserted for over a century. Its story is typical of so many Pennine villages. Agricultural decline, the shift of handloom weaving to the mills and the flooding of the valley to create reservoirs in the 19th century meant a dispersal of population. Ruined farms now dominate the moorland scene.

This walk is a circular route round the area of Haslingden Grane and follows hillside paths on both sides of the Ogden Valley. A few ascents of steep slopes are encountered on the walk.

The Duke of Wellington

The pub is situated halfway along the walk route but does provide an alternative start/finish point for the walk. The roadside hostelry named after the Iron Duke offers all the quality and variety in a menu we have come to expect from a Brewer's Fayre establishment. Boddingtons bitter is served here, with popular traditional dishes like gammon, steak and kidney pie, half roasted chicken and chilli con carne. Not to mention a wide range of excellent desserts. Food is served all day and there are plenty of facilities here, including a beer garden which overlooks the Ogden Valley and provides fine moorland views.

Telephone: 01706 215610.

The Walk

①Cross the stile to the left of the information centre to reach another stile. Follow the wall side steeply uphill to another stile on the left. Do not cross it but turn right and follow a faint path running parallel to a wall, heading in the direction of a ruin and a clump of mature trees. Cross a stile at the next fence line and continue in the same direction with the quarry in view over to the right. The path drops down to a footbridge then climbs the hillside on the other side of a little valley. Follow the waymarkers and keep the quarry fence on the right. When the fence changes direction, bear right to another ruined farmhouse by a Rossendale Way marker post. Cross the stile by the gate here and follow the track downhill to meet the quarry access road.

②Turn left and follow the access road to

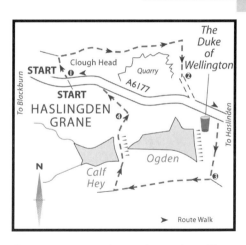

the cottages on the main road at Heap Clough. Turn left and follow the busy A road for about 250 yards until the Duke of Wellington is reached on the opposite side of the road. Take great care crossing this fast road. The walk continues from the pub by continuing downhill along the pavement for about 50 yards, then joining a path at a stile on the right hand side of the road. Follow the path downhill to the reservoir, cross a ladder stile and turn right. Turn left in front of a gate, cross a footbridge and follow the path uphill alongside the fence to reach another stile.

PLACES OF INTEREST NEARBY

The **Clough Head information centre** is open weekends and bank holidays in summer and on Sundays in winter (telephone: 01706 830162). Only a few miles down the road from here there is a chance to experience the heyday of Lancashire's Industrial Revolution. **The Helmshore Textile Museums** (telephone: 01706 226459), south of Haslingden, house revolutionary textile machines like Hargreaves' spinning jenny and Arkwright's water-frame. See working Victorian looms in action in their old mill setting and recapture the days when cotton was king!

Looking down the Grane Valley towards Haslingden

③ Turn right here and follow the path for about ³/₄ mile, skirting the hillside above Ogden Reservoir to reach Calf Hey Reservoir. Join the dam wall of this reservoir by dropping down from the hillside at a kissing gate by a solitary tree. Follow the path along the dam wall and, on the far side, go through a gate and bear right along a drive which leads to a car park.

④ Head for the car park entrance but join a woodland path on the left before the entrance is reached. The path is signed for Clough Head car park and information centre. Follow this path between a fence and trees overlooking the road. This path leads back to the busy A6177. Cross this again with great care, follow the verge for a very short distance then go through a gate on the right which leads back to the information centre through woodland.

Tockholes
The Royal Arms

DIRECTIONS TO START: THE STARTING POINT IS A MILE SOUTH OF TOCKHOLES VILLAGE, ROUGHLY HALFWAY ALONG THE MINOR ROAD LINKING BLACKBURN (A6062) WITH BELMONT (A675). **PARKING:** THE WEST PENNINE MOORS CAR PARK ADJACENT TO THE ROYAL ARMS PUB AND RODDLESWORTH INFORMATION CENTRE.

Tockholes is a straggling moorland community made up of isolated farmsteads and roadside cottages once occupied by handloom weavers. The rocket-ship shape of Darwen (Jubilee) Tower dominates the moors hereabouts – a folly erected on the spur of a hill in 1897 to celebrate Queen Victoria's Diamond Jubilee. The Roddlesworth Valley was flooded by Liverpool Corporation in the 1850s, leading to the demise of Hollinshead Hall – once the manor house of Tockholes.

The walk is a shady woodland stroll to the ruins of Hollinshead Hall, then returns along the valley to the upper reaches of Roddlesworth Reservoir. There is one steep ascent out of the valley at the end of the walk. But persevere, as the pub is at the top of the hill!

The Royal Arms

This small functional hostelry was designed for local rural folk but now attracts the urban populations of the nearby towns on their days out in the country. The visitor information centre and recreational woodlands of the Roddlesworth Valley bring walkers and riders to this honeypot – particularly at weekends – and the car park is a starting point for the popular ascent of nearby Darwen Tower. The cosy Royal Arms thrives on the trade and offers a warm welcome to drinkers and diners. Food is served every day from 12 noon until 8 pm and Mitchell's beers (rare in South Lancashire) are complemented by ales like Wadworth 6X and Everards Tiger. Telephone: 01254 705373.

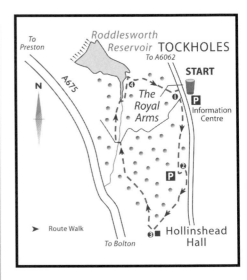

The Walk

① Turn left out of the car park, cross the bus terminus and go through the gates on the opposite side of the road, signed for Roddlesworth Reservoirs. Do not go as far as the waymarker post but almost immediately turn left and follow a faint path into woodland. This path runs parallel to the wall and the road. Keep the wall on the left and the path eventually bears right and reaches a stile in a fence. Cross the stile and continue in the same direction along a faint boggy path which eventually leads into a car park.

② Turn left along the car park access and just before the road is reached turn right through a gate in the wall. Follow the path which now runs alongside the wall and the road. It soon swings right and runs downhill as a grassy path which leads into the ruins of Hollinshead Hall, once the manor house for the village of Tockholes. An information panel outlines the history of the site. Don't forget to visit the nearby Well House which is thought to be on the site of a mystic shrine – reputedly haunted!

③ Turn right out of the ruins along a gravel path which forks into two by a wall. Take the right fork which climbs uphill to a gate. Keep going straight ahead along a stone bridleway which drops downhill to reach a shady footbridge over a stream. Cross the footbridge and immediately go through the metal kissing gate on the right hand side of the bridge to continue the walk alongside the stream. Follow the path through the wooded valley until another footbridge is crossed and then walk with the stream on the left. Keep going straight ahead at the junction of paths, following a wooden fence until the upper shore of the reservoir is reached.

The haunted Well House of Hollinshead Hall

④ At the bench offering a view down the reservoir turn right and follow the

PLACES OF INTEREST NEARBY

The **Roddlesworth information centre** (telephone: 01254 704502) provides details of walks and trails in the local area. For an indoor treat, head for nearby Chorley and visit the antiques mecca and craft centre of **Botany Bay** (telephone: 01257 261220) where you can rustle through old books, buy craft materials and admire the old tanks and fire engines.

waymarked nature trail uphill, leaving the reservoir behind you. At the next path junction continue straight ahead uphill along the path signed for the nature trail and information centre. The path becomes quite steep and opens out to a view of the moors. Near the top of the hill, take the path forking left which climbs steps and leads to the road with the front door of the pub directly opposite. Turn right to go back to the car park.

Croston
The Lord Nelson

MAP: EXPLORER 285 SOUTHPORT & CHORLEY (GR 489186)

WALK 26

DISTANCE: $3\frac{1}{4}$ MILES

DIRECTIONS TO START: START BY THE VILLAGE GREEN IN THE CENTRE OF CROSTON WHICH IS SITUATED ON THE A581 HALFWAY BETWEEN SOUTHPORT AND CHORLEY. **PARKING:** THERE IS A SMALL PARKING AREA BY THE VILLAGE GREEN IN FRONT OF THE LORD NELSON.

Bustling 'cross-town', a farming village built around an ancient holy cross, was for centuries the market centre for the extensive mosslands stretching westward to the sea. The existence of a large number of inns testifies to this former importance. Warm red-brick 18th century houses and cobbled streets are the predominant feature of Croston. The original settlement was founded upon a crossing point of the River Yarrow, a less well-known Lancashire river which rises in the Chorley foothills and meanders westward to join the River Douglas.

This gentle walk is ideal for families as it is entirely flat so there is little chance of anyone complaining about steep gradients! It leaves the River Yarrow behind and wanders over Croston Moss along farm tracks before returning to the ancient heart of the village.

The Lord Nelson

With its pleasant situation overlooking the village green, the Lord Nelson lays claim to being the oldest inn in Croston. This popular local is small, cosy and countrified, exuding a rural charm as it harks back to Croston's farming heyday. Bar and restaurant meals are available here every day at lunchtimes and in the evenings. Beers include Boddingtons Bitter and Higsons Bitter. Telephone: 01772 600387.

The River Yarrow flows through Croston

The Walk

① From the village green turn right in front of the Wheatsheaf inn and cross over the main road. By the teashop, turn left along the lane signed as Castle Walks. Go straight ahead along the tarmac path which leads to a footbridge over the River Yarrow. Cross this and continue straight ahead along the gravel drive past houses. Turn right and follow the pavement, then left at the next T-junction of roads. Follow Drinkhouse Lane which swings right and reaches open fields beyond cottages. It eventually swings left and continues as a private road.

② Go straight ahead along this farm access road and after about ¹/₂ mile farm buildings are reached at a junction of tracks. Continue straight ahead here along the track, which offers extensive

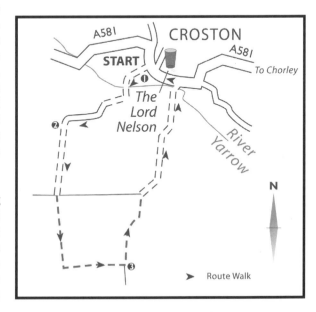

Track across Croston Moss

views across the Moss to the West Pennine Moors, including Winter Hill. Shortly after passing a derelict red-brick barn, look out for an adjoining track on the left signed with a yellow waymarker. Turn left and follow this track between fields until it meets another track running in a north-south direction.

③ Turn left and head back towards the grand looking house straight ahead. When this house is passed on the left, turn right then left along the tarmac lane between hedges. This route, Carr Lane, is followed for about $1/2$ mile and heads back towards the village church. The pretty red-brick houses of the village are soon reached.

Turn right over another cobbled bridge over the River Yarrow to reach the high street opposite the Grapes pub. Turn left to return to the village green.

PLACES OF INTEREST NEARBY

Across the West Lancashire Plain at Burscough, **Martin Mere** (telephone: 01704 895181) is a popular nature reserve managed by the Wildfowl and Wetlands Trust. Exotic ducks, flamingos, pink-footed geese and koi carp are just a small selection of the wildlife to be encountered here and the lakes attract endangered species of migrating waterfowl. There is also a visitor garden and a children's adventure playground.

Heskin Green
The Farmer's Arms

MAP: EXPLORER 285 SOUTHPORT & CHORLEY (GR 533154)

WALK 27

DISTANCE: $2^3/_4$ MILES

DIRECTIONS TO START: THE VILLAGE IS SITUATED ON THE B5250 JUST SOUTH OF ECCLESTON AND NORTH OF JUNCTION 27 ON THE M6 AT STANDISH. **PARKING:** THE FARMER'S ARMS ON THE B5250 HAS A LARGE CAR PARK (PATRONS) BUT THERE IS NO PARKING ON THE ROAD HERE AS IT IS CLOSE TO A JUNCTION ON THE BEND OF A ROAD.

The busy M6 cuts a fast dash through rural West Lancashire allowing heavy traffic to avoid the back roads through tiny settlements like Heskin Green. This roadside community is still busy with passers-by though, thanks largely to the popular Camelot Theme Park which has sprung up in the fields north of the village, leaving cows to look on bemused. The road through the old farming settlement also provides a convenient shortcut between the motorway and the larger commuter villages of West Lancashire. Amidst all this modernity are quiet lanes and an intricate network of footpaths and bridleways which linked the many old farmsteads across a patchwork of small hedged fields.

Old farms and houses like Howe Brook House and Heskin Hall are passed along this level walk which follows paths, lanes and farm tracks. Elegant Heskin Hall is open to the public as an antique centre.

The Farmer's Arms

Formerly known as the 'Pleasant Retreat', the Farmer's Arms may have changed its title (since 1902) but in every respect still remains true to its original name. This inn is an intriguing delight not to be missed, from the ivy-entwined floral abundance of the beer garden to the curiosity-clad interior bedecked with horse collars, prints, horns and brasses reflecting the bygone days of local farming. The 18th century roadside hostelry once housed a stables and it still welcomes horse riders and ramblers today as well as the more noticeable car-borne travellers. The varied standard menu, complemented by blackboard specials (like Steak Diane and Drambuie Pork), offers starters such as Prawn Neptune, salads with meats from the local butcher, mixed grills and the popular steak pie dish – affectionately known as the 'Farmer's Favourite'. There is also an extensive sweet menu. With a relaxing vault for wearers of muddy boots, a restaurant and overnight accommodation, the Farmer's Arms has something for everyone – including weekly guest ales that join beers like Timothy Taylor Landlord, Castle Eden, Flowers IPA and Trophy Cask. Food is served every day from 12 noon until 9.30 pm (9 pm on Sundays). Telephone: 01257 451276.

The Walk

① Pass in front of the pub and go down the track which runs down the side of it to a little footbridge. Cross it and walk uphill to join a lane. Turn right on this lane and follow it past houses until a T-junction is reached. Turn right and follow Withington Lane which soon leads to another T-junction opposite the village shop. Turn left here along the pavement and after a short distance take care and cross over to a stile in the hedge on the right hand side of the road where a signed footpath is indicated.

② Go over this stile and walk straight ahead through the field, crossing a drain to reach a stile on the opposite side of the field. Cross this and follow the field edge to reach a track. Go straight ahead along the track and continue straight ahead across a stile when the track swings left. Go straight ahead in the next field, keeping the hedge side to your right. On the far side of this field there are two access points. Follow the one on the left over a stream and continue in the same direction with the hedge on your right. Cross two more stiles to reach a narrow, hedged lane.

③ Turn right along the minor lane and soon after it swings right it meets a track signed as a public footpath and public bridleway. Turn left and follow this grassy track which swings left to a gate, then

PLACES OF INTEREST NEARBY

Just up the road in **Eccleston** is the large antiques and memorabilia complex, **Bygone Times** (telephone: 01257 451889), crammed with nostalgic artefacts. A contrasting family venue is also close at hand if you turn right (if going north) at the road junction by the Farmer's Arms. This leads to **Camelot Theme Park** (telephone: 01257 452100) where you can go on a rollercoaster – preferably not after a big pub lunch!

Elegant Heskin Hall

turns right and reaches the derelict buildings of a historic farmhouse. Walk through the site and bear left to reach a road. Turn right along this for a very short distance before almost immediately turning right along a footpath by a farm gate. This tarmac farm road is now followed for $^1/_2$ mile to reach the B road and along the way Heskin Hall is passed on the left. Continue along the drive past the Hall to reach the road.

④ Turn right on the busy B road and follow the pavement for about $^1/_4$ mile until the road bends sharp right by a junction. Follow the road around to the right until the pub is reached on the opposite side of the road. Take great care crossing at this road bend to reach the pub.

Belmont
The Belmont Bull

MAP: EXPLORER 287 WEST PENNINE MOORS (GR 674163)

WALK 28

DISTANCE: 2½ MILES

DIRECTIONS TO START: THE VILLAGE IS 6 MILES NORTH OF BOLTON ON THE A675.
PARKING: ROADSIDE PARKING ALONG THE VILLAGE MAIN STREET.

Belmont probably epitomises the outsiders' idea of a typical Lancashire village, with its 19th century mill workers' stone cottages. Straggling a lonely moorland road, it is surrounded by high hills, not to mention reservoirs and mill lodges which originally provided a water supply for the village's textile industry. The name of the village translates as 'beautiful hill' and though the moors hereabouts can appear quite menacing in rough weather – particularly the ominous steep scarp of Winter Hill – Belmont really does occupy a pleasant situation.

The lonely moorland wilderness just a stone's throw from the village is revealed by this short walk. A track across rough pasture in the shadow of Winter Hill is followed. Then a moorland road leads down to the popular summer honeypot of a reservoir locally known as the 'blue lagoon'.

The Belmont Bull

Up until recent years this large, imposing hostelry on the village main street was known as the Black Bull. The new name reinforces its associations with the village and the Bull offers a warm welcome to all. Food is available at lunchtimes and in the evenings with Sunday lunch specials and the beers on offer include Matthew Brown Bitter. Telephone: 01204 811370.

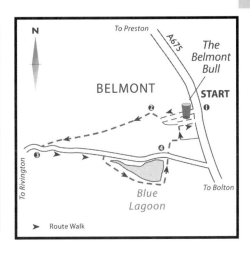

The Walk

① On the upper side of the Belmont Bull walk along Chapel Street next to the inn. Beyond the cottages continue along the track straight ahead which soon reveals the moorland reservoir and the masts of Winter Hill. By the bench bear right to a gate and stile. Cross the stile and continue along the grassy track with the fence on the right until stone steps in a wall are reached.

Belmont's 'blue lagoon'

② Cross over the wall and bear left along a grass path with the high masts over to the left. The path heads gradually uphill, passes through a gap in a wall and becomes increasingly boggy. It runs parallel to the road over to the left and eventually meets it at a stile.

③ Turn left and walk downhill along the road in the direction of the village church. The road is now followed for about $1/2$ mile. After passing a rough car parking area above the reservoir cross a drain by a roadside wall and turn right off the road along a path which drops downhill and bears left to footbridges. When the path forks into two by a bridge over the stream, take the right fork and follow the path with the stream to your left. The path then runs around the reservoir and crosses a bridge to rejoin the road.

④ Cross the road and, directly opposite, cross a stile and continue straight ahead between a fence and wall. At the junction of the tracks turn right between the playing field and allotments. When the first house is reached on the right turn left at a gap in the wall and follow an enclosed track uphill to the end of a cul-de-sac. Turn right here to rejoin the main street alongside the inn.

PLACES OF INTEREST NEARBY

Continue westwards along the lonely moorland road up past the 'blue lagoon' to reach **Rivington** village. The car park and information centre at **Rivington Great House Barn** is the ideal base from which to explore the paths alongside reservoirs at Lever Park. Head uphill through the ornamental gardens laid out by Lord Leverhulme to reach the moorland folly of Rivington Pike. The information centre (telephone: 01254 691549) also has a café and shop.

Entwistle
The Strawbury Duck

MAP: EXPLORER 287 WEST PENNINE MOORS (GR 723173)   **WALK 29**   **DISTANCE:** 2 MILES

DIRECTIONS TO START: LEAVE THE B6391, WHICH RUNS BETWEEN CHAPELTOWN VILLAGE AND THE A666, AT THE MINOR LANE SIGNED AS BATRIDGE ROAD. THIS ROAD ENDS AT ENTWISTLE RESERVOIR.
PARKING: START THE WALK AT THE RESERVOIR CAR PARK WHICH IS $^1/_2$ MILE AWAY FROM THE PUB.

Entwistle is hardly a village. It is barely even a hamlet. But it is well known to anglers, commuters and beer drinkers thanks to three things: its reservoir, its train station and the popular Strawbury Duck. A fine row of railway cottages nestles around the inn. Otherwise it is a loose collection of farmsteads at the upper end of the Bradshaw Valley which was flooded in the 19th century to provide water for mills and later for the burgeoning town of Bolton.

The walk skirts the wooded shorelines of Entwistle Reservoir (1838) and Wayoh Reservoir (1876). The route also passes under an impressive Victorian viaduct which carries the Bolton-Blackburn railway high over the valley.

The Strawbury Duck

Hidden away at the end of a moorland backroad, the telescope, street lamp and red phone box that adorn the outside of the Strawbury Duck are a curiosity in themselves. But the greater surprise is the pub itself – perhaps the most talked about country pub in Lancashire – an award winning hostelry that turns up in all sorts of national pub and heritage guides … including this one! So what's so special? The name itself – this was formerly the Station Hotel built in 1900 – keeps people guessing. Then there's the location – tucked away in the back of beyond. But it's inside that the Strawbury Duck unveils its real attractions. Simply furnished with stone floors and wooden beams, the pub lets its food, ale and clientele do the talking. There's a standard menu and daily specials that will fill the stomach of even the hungriest rambler. Soup, baguettes, assorted pies, whitebait, venison and the tasty sausages and mash (various flavours) are just a few of the treats on offer. Then there's the beer – a wide range of real ales such as Timothy Taylor Landlord and Moorhouse's Pendle Witches Brew and the appropriate Ramblers Winter Warmer (served in winter, naturally). Food is available at lunchtimes and in the evenings every day. Telephone: 01204 852013.

The Walk

① Starting from the car park entrance turn right and follow the drive over the embankment towards the opposite corner

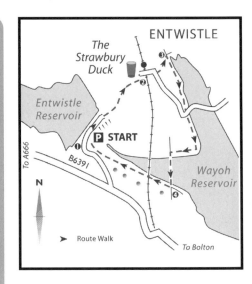

of the reservoir. Continue along the drive which runs uphill past a camping barn on the left. It becomes a rough road and leads past a row of cottages to the Strawbury Duck.

② Turn right along the road at the front of the inn and cross the road bridge over the railway by the train station. Follow the road around to the right from where there is a good view looking eastwards to Holcombe Moor. Almost immediately on the left, go through the little wooden gate waymarked with a yellow arrow and drop down through the field to a stile. Cross this and follow the path through woodland until a bench is reached on the right just before a footbridge.

③ Do not cross the bridge but turn right by the bench to follow a woodland path. The inlet to Wayoh Reservoir is soon seen on the left and the path is followed straight ahead until it reaches a kissing gate by a road. Go directly across the road to pass through another gate and

The 'highlands' encircling Entwistle Reservoir

continue along the shoreline of the reservoir. The path bears right and soon reaches a spur of the reservoir. Follow the path which crosses the reservoir along an embankment.

④ When the railings end on the far side of the embankment, turn sharp right immediately to follow an adjoining path. This wooded path is signed as a concessionary route for Entwistle embankment car park and leads under the mighty viaduct. Keep high above the steep sided valley and as you approach a gate look out for a yellow waymarker post to the right.

Follow this and steps downhill lead back to the car park.

PLACES OF INTEREST NEARBY

Two historic houses can be found nearby on the north side of Bolton. Just south along the B6391 is **Turton Tower** (telephone: 01204 852203), parts of which date back to 1420. With Civil War connections and having been the home of industrialist James Kay it contains artefacts from Tudor, Stuart and Victorian times. Head a bit further south from here to reach **Hall i' th' Wood** (telephone: 01204 301159), another museum, which was the birthplace of Samuel Crompton the inventor of the Spinning Mule.

Holcombe
The Shoulder of Mutton

<table>
<tr><td>MAP: EXPLORER 287 WEST PENNINE MOORS (GR 782184)</td><td>WALK 30</td><td>DISTANCE: 4½ MILES</td></tr>
</table>

DIRECTIONS TO START: HOLCOMBE MOOR STRETCHES NORTH FROM THE VILLAGE OF HOLCOMBE WHICH IS ½ MILE NORTH OF HOLCOMBE BROOK, AT THE SOUTHERN END OF THE B6214.
PARKING: START THE WALK AT THE SMALL FREE CAR PARK SITUATED ON THE WESTERN SIDE OF THE B6214 A MILE NORTH OF HOLCOMBE VILLAGE.

The 1970s' administrative boundary changes dumped the tiny moorland community of Holcombe into the metropolitan county of Greater Manchester. It has now become fashionable commuter territory but its roots lie in the traditional sheep farming of the Rossendale uplands. In the 19th century the distinct landmark of Peel Tower was erected to celebrate the repeal of the Corn Laws in 1852. Robert Peel was then Prime Minister and was also locally born, in nearby Bury.

This walk starts at the administrative edge of the post-1974 county of Lancashire and climbs Holcombe Moor to pass the Pilgrim's Cross memorial stone and Peel Tower which is a breathtaking viewpoint across the Manchester conurbation. It drops to the stone cottages of Holcombe village and the pub before returning to the car park along the old moorland highway which ran north to Rossendale.

The Shoulder of Mutton

The stark, stone grey exterior of the Shoulder of Mutton is uninvitingly sombre. But head inside to discover a Lancashire classic – a warm and friendly roadside hostelry whose reputation for quality food ensures the pub car park is always full. The spacious old-fashioned interior of wooden seats and tables is largely arranged around a fireplace with a crackling log fire in winter, overlooked from the bar. There is also a separate restaurant, but most intriguing and inviting of all is the dark and curious little side room adorned with an eclectic collection of original sketches and portraits of subjects including Peel Tower, Irish characters and Manchester United players! There is a large selection of bitters, amongst which are Timothy Taylor, Theakstons, John Smith's, Tetley and IPA. The Shoulder of Mutton is a pub which proves difficult to leave. Especially if you have had a rack or shoulder of lamb – the most appropriate dish in a pub with sheep 'connections'. Food is all home cooked and traditional and is available at lunchtimes and in the evenings on Monday to Friday (though not Monday night) and from 12 noon until 9 pm at weekends. Dogs are also very welcome here. Telephone: 01706 822001.

The Walk

① At the car park entrance facing the road, turn left and follow the permissive path which runs parallel to the road. This leads to an adjoining footpath. Turn left along this and climb steeply uphill to a

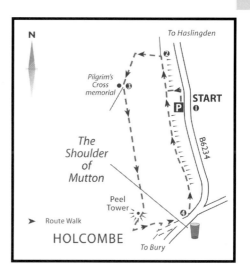

farm. Turn right on the adjoining wide track which was an old moorland road. Follow it until a high wall and woodland are reached by a ladder stile on your right.

② At this point turn left where there is a rough assortment of tracks. Climb onto the moors here along a path which runs with walls to the left and right. Head for the top corner of the wall on the left and another path is reached. Bear left to a Rifle Range notice (taking heed of the warning). Keep to this path which runs uphill past further notices to reach the stone memorial recording the site of the Pilgrim's Cross (which existed in the 12th century) on top of a moorland plateau.

③ Continue straight ahead across the open moor, heading directly for Peel Tower, the top of which can be seen in the distance. The path runs across the flat moorland top, then drops downhill and crosses a stream and the Tower is reached after about a mile. Admire the extensive views from the Tower, then continue ahead along the track in front of it. The

Heading down to Holcombe Church

track zig zags downhill and reaches a cobbled lane. Turn left along this past elegant stone houses and it soon meets the road almost opposite the Shoulder of Mutton. Bear left and cross over to reach the pub.

④ From the pub go up the track between the stone buildings that are opposite the pub car park. This climbs gradually uphill and goes over a cattle grid. This wide track past farmsteads is now followed for the next mile, running parallel to the valley below. Eventually it reaches the farm buildings passed near the start of the walk. Turn right here and walk downhill to rejoin the path leading back to the car park.

PLACES OF INTEREST NEARBY

Ramsbottom is just down the hill from Holcombe and is an interesting mix of antique and craft shops. It is also a train halt on the **East Lancashire Steam Railway** (telephone: 0161 7647790) which runs weekend steam trains along the restored line from Bury to Rawtenstall.